A LEAP OF FAITH

A LIFE FILLED WITH QUESTIONABLE CHOICES

Anita L. Helm

For Mom, through God,
you took care of Nita

CONTENTS

ACKNOWLEDGEMENTS

All thanks to Jesus Christ, the First and the Last, the Beginning and the End.

I can't say enough about my mom, the true foundation of the woman I am today. My gratefulness to God is forever for the love and friendship of Rev. William D. Helm (aka Rev). Great thanks and love to my daughters Albani and Faith. Thank you, Broderick, my son-in-law, and your parents Neil and Beverly. A lifetime of love for my siblings Yvonne, Clara, and Aaron (aka Bush) and your spouses: Roscoe, William (Cookie), and Nancy. My love to my Helm family: David, Bridget, and Darlene (never forgotten: Joyce and Timmy). Endless love and gratitude to Pam and Tina, my sister-nieces, and their husbands (Kyle and Gilbert). I treasure you all. No words for the unfailing generosity and love from Lillie, Bud, Alice, Faye, Brenda, and Bob. You all have given peace and comfort toward Mom and Aunt Ann. Aunt Ann I am grateful to have you in my life. To my inner circle: Pam, Theresa, Ledora, Angie, and Beth, thanks for all you all are to me. Love and a lifetime of collaboration to Matt and Mike. I pray heavenly rewards for my spiritual parents Bill and Diana Lee. Thanks to my extended village: the RBC Family, the Orlando Crew, Tanya, Greg, Mary, Priscilla, Fayre, Michelle, Blenn, Rich, Herb, and Frank. Hugs to all my tremendous family and friends. Know that I say your names in my heart and in my prayers. Last but not least, my four-legged bundle of energy – Momma loves you Yoshi.

PREFACE

For some time now, I have wanted to write a story about my life. I'm still living, so this is my capture of my first half. I hope the stories will help you know we all have a story worth telling. The reality is this book is not about glamour, my persona, or me covering up for my messes. My truth is learning to love me regardless of what people think. People pleasing has influenced many of the bad, questionable, and ill-advised choices in my life. I want to be open about my own charade and help people learn to feel and live unguardedly. Sounds easy, but it certainly is *not*!

The title of this book, *A Leap of Faith: A Life Filled with Questionable Choices*, is relatable to many. This is how I settled on it. As I watched a young boy learning to swim, I saw his little body bent over, his toes gripping the side of the pool and moving to strangle his instructor's neck. He jumped! Whether it was the instructor who pulled or the child who relented, I will never know.

The boy dragged his waterlogged frame up the cement steps to his Dad's embrace. After all of it, his face exploded with joy that was quickly replaced with a burst of tears. His tears expressed that was too much! *What kind of people love me?*

Seeing that moment play out and asking myself what kind of people love me was how I got my book title. We all take leaps one at a time. I understood that boy. I understood that confusion. I understood about the things we do for the people we love. I could relate to that lad's leap. The writing of my stories began with questions from my daughters, Albani and Faith. As part of a Christmas gift, they sent me questions about my life. In answering their questions, I realized they wanted more than personal anecdotes. They wanted to understand what the future held for them in so many areas. What was the makeup, the journey, and the constitution, of my womanhood? What made my womanhood work or fail? What were its phases? They had so many questions. I could see those two young women wanting to understand their mother's rite of passage, her journey to womanhood. Their questions sought to have me, their Mom, unravel mysteries that college and their experience hadn't taught them. If I couldn't help their uncertainty, who could?

As I crafted my words early on, I knew I wanted to share beyond my own children. Many of us, whether men or women, hit upon uncertainty during our own rites of passage. We seldom have a ceremony to say, "Hey, you arrived." There aren't manuals to tell us who we are and what we are sent here to do. I have shared the intimate collection of my many personal leaps and what answers about my life have come from them. I want to inspire persistence, hope, and resilience in my readers. All of us are on a quest in life, and in life no one size fits all.

Going into the deep with me, you should know starting out that my leaps of faith didn't all end badly. Some leaps landed squarely on beds of pillows, but a heck of a lot of them splashed down face-first on the pavement! Regardless, I lived to tell the tale. God got me through the dismounts and the brokenness. My leaps have been terrifying and thrilling. I can't remove any one of them because, collectively, they make me, Anita, who I am. You have your leaps and I have mine. Whatever you decide to do, remember we all leap off the side of life's pool without knowing how we will land. Keep hope during the fall.

LAUNCH PAD I: THE GIRL WITH THE BRIGHT SMILE

The Winepress

My Mom's name is Rosetta Bush. Rose Bush. Her maiden name was Thornton. Thorny Rose Bush. How cool a name for her. I asked about the origin of my name, and she said she picked Anita from the first page of a baby book. How's that for not being original? *Thanks, Mom.* As a child, I didn't have a cool name, or much else. The name Anita wasn't cool, so I got the nickname Nita.

I have had a lot of sweet moments in my life and others that would make me say "Sugar Tang " in place "F U" (I'm not a big curser).

I'm the baby of a blended family of four, and the other three are colorful in their own lanes. Their names are Yvonne, Clara, and Aaron. I call my older brother, Bush.

Since childhood, I have been everyone else's cheerleader and not always my own. My early start was fostered from the dust of a dirt road. I start you off with insignificant things to prepare you that from my entry into life, I didn't feel significant.

Because of crushing experiences in childhood I looked at life as though the glass was half empty. You wouldn't know it to look at me. Back then I was a little chubby, round-cheeked girl who didn't have much to say. But when I said something, I was bossy and in charge. That much hasn't changed. For the most part, I seemed positive.

Behind the outward façade, something else was brewing. The Anita of my early years was darker and terrified. If God had not interrupted my life, I doubt I would be the positive force I am today. I just know I would have been different.

Like most kids, I coped with emotions using food and TV. I have always loved to talk, teach, and laugh. Those have been my outlets. I longed for something in my life—I just didn't know what. It constantly nagged at me.

I was born to an unlikely pairing of two opposites. My Dad, William "Bill" Bush, was an old man, born in 1910. My Mom, Rosie, was born in 1929. That's a nineteen-year age gap. Dad was high yellow from the West Indies and Mom was dark ebony from Northern Virginia. Back then, color codes would have called him cream to her coffee. Neither of them was well educated, but both were smart. What a peculiar time and space God used for the mystery of me. My surprise 1967 arrival was as remarkable as it was unpredictable. My Dad was kissing fifty-seven, in remission from lung cancer, a drinker, and an average Joe when I came.

Bill Bush was ahead of his time. He was a thinker and strategist before such terms were associated with colored men of his era. What my

Dad lacked in education, privilege, and good health; he made up for in making his small life bigger.

He put energy toward his ambitions. He saw opportunities and took them. He started his own concrete patio business with only a primary education. He was a survivor and made up his rules as he went along. He and his beer-guzzling friends were laborers—that is, they were reliable for a good patio before the bottles were opened. They all had hearts of gold and doted on Bill's baby girl, Nita. I was an old man's princess.

I don't know a lot about my Dad. Even the fact that he came from the West Indies I know only by word of mouth. What I reflect on now is mixed with truth and projections from my childhood memories. Mom would yell at him that he was spoiling me. I remember eating bad snacks, and that after one scream of "Daddy," he would rescue me from every situation.

We had potato-chip-eating adventures in his old beat-up station wagon. My Dad was fun. His station wagon was always loaded down with concrete bags, buckets, shovels, levels, and junk. My Mom never allowed any of that stuff into her nicely cleaned house. The tools found themselves under our house in a dark and creepy crawl space. I hated that crawl space! If Dad was too tired, he would ask me to walk the levels and shovels under there. The place was scary, and I was afraid snakes would eat me. I dragged that stuff in and ran out fast!

In my childlike honesty, I often messed up Dad's schemes. My mouth would possibly sabotage his pulling a fast one over on a vendor. Here is a memory of a TV return. Our new color TV blew out during a lightning storm. Dad and I went to town to take the TV back. As Dad was explaining that the TV didn't work, he omitted an important part of the story.

I grabbed his trousers. "Daddy, tell 'em 'bout the lightning."

He pushed me off and kept talking.

"Daddy, don't forget about the lightning!"

He brushed me off for the final time. The guy didn't know what I was going on about. As the story ended, we walked out of the store with a new color TV. Turns out the lightning was not significant after all.

My Dad was a man of charm, cunning, and great charisma. He was half bald and stood 6'1" with a *bright* smile. For the most part, he wore sweat-stained T-shirts, spackle-spotted khaki pants, and his beaming smile for everyone he met. Working hard was his swagger. When he and my Mom shined up, they looked like movie stars. He built our home with his own hands before big machines and gadgets. Any excess lumber or supplies from his construction jobs found their way into our home. Taking care of his family was his life. To this day I wish I grew up in the age of having a camera to take pictures clearer than my foggy memories. His videos would have been priceless. My kids could have seen their grandaddy in action.

The fun times were few, the suffering vast. I saw from childhood to eleven years old hospitals, sick people, and incomprehensible things. Life's opening round for Anita Bush was a sucker punch to the gut. Words like *cancer* weren't spoken back then. Practices like hospice for poor black people were *not* available back then. From late 1978 to January 1979, my Dad lay in bed, dying by himself, with me, a latchkey kid, coming home to play his nursemaid. I recall the many days I walked into the kitchen and yelled, "Dad, Dad, Dad!" hoping to hear him respond.

I didn't know a lot, but by sixth grade, I felt he could die soon, and I'd be the one to find him. I would round the corner of the hall to look into the dark room. I would see him lying there motionless. The covers and his chest hardly moved. Finally he'd flinch, and I would know he wasn't dead. I could breathe again.

I would then warm up a can of pea soup. That was the only thing he could keep down. Oftentimes, he ate nothing all day. He barely existed. I lived those terror-filled moments every day for weeks.

Before he got so sick, I could get him to eat a little, help him to the bedside toilet, and run and get him a cigarette. I wanted to do something, anything to help him. I would watch as the unnamed sickness destroyed him. There were too many gross things to speak about. The sickness destroyed his body, his swagger and did many abnormal things.

I witnessed my giant of a father shrivel to pint size. In the end, you subconsciously wish for the suffering to stop. You don't wish for your Dad to die, but you want his torture to end. As a child, you don't know there is no ending the torture without ending him. No torture, no Dad.

Decades after his death, my kids asked me what I admired about my Dad. I found the question off-putting and disorienting. I never reached back to the winepress of those hidden memories. The child who was terrified to turn the door handle for fear of finding a dead body left those thoughts far behind. The woman Anita left a lot of my childhood behind. I'd reflect on big wheels, playing, and the fun of my childhood, but not on Dad. When I escape a horror, I don't take drive-bys even with my memories.

My Dad gave me life, my smile, and my love for possibilities. When people react to my smile, I think of my Dad. The irony is he and my Mom wore dentures. They both lost all their teeth early in life. I remember that cautionary tale and brush my teeth all the time. God has let me keep a mouthful.

Unlikely Pairing

Growing up without a Dad in much of my life has had an impact. There are vulnerabilities I didn't know to watch out for. I know of them now because I fell into traps back then. I had moments and gaps that having a man in my life would have helped me navigate. I leaped into situations that on the surface looked safe but were deadly.

With both my parents there were fractures. Their love and attraction was a mystery. They were opposites. Even though I didn't experience their relationship of marriage for long, as a child I could see their differences. I saw my Mom, a risk-adverse woman maneuvering and fighting. She married my Dad, a fearless and sometimes reckless risk-taker. He unsettled her.

My Dad loved track races. His ill-fated bad checks would race his money to the bank every week. Dad hoped his deposits were faster than the bank's check processing. When the bank was faster, my Mom would pitch a fit. She had lungs over money, especially mismanagement of it.

The biggest fights my parents had were over those damn checks dribbling all over town. That's the only time I heard her lose it. I had no idea at the time how basketball and checks had any connection.

My Mom did not like to play games with money. You either had it or you didn't. She was a saver and a banker. She cataloged every penny and could locate a two-cent error in her bank register. She went from cleaning houses, caring for White rich children, working in restaurants, to working as a bank loan processor. She made little to no money, but she was a professional. That was a big accomplishment to her.

These two very different generations lived and loved under one roof. My Dad's almost twenty-year seniority didn't seem to faze them until he took sick. She carried on life for them both through sickness and in health.

Death didn't bring calm to our home; it brought *finality*. During the many hospital visits, the sickness, the drugs, the gross stuff like eye ooze, bandages, and toilet guk—my mother kept her house clean and the refrigerator full and never missed church. She demonstrated caregiving at a master's level.

Little did I know what lessons would be repeated. Before a hurricane there is a quiet calm before the whistling of the freight train of destruction. That's how death hit our small home and my tiny existence. No one told me to anchor down. No one warned me my life was going to be turned upside down. Nothing about the two people God used to get me here should have worked, but God's mission was accomplished. I was born.

William Bush went home to be with the Lord on January 15, 1979. The most unlikely pairing had finally been separated. *Till death do us part.* They honored that.

The Aftermath of the Press

God didn't wait until I was fully grown before taking my Dad. He shattered my innocence. I was pummeled while still sprouting. I learned about death before enjoying life. I'm not sure who does that. *God did.* Grief is profound enough for the fully formed and unimaginable for the young. Kids like me who experience death in our childhood need some special attention from God in our lifetime. God allowed our worlds to be shattered before we were firmly footed. The sucker punch of my opening round was crushing. It felt unfair. Its sting reached into my womanhood. I'm more reserved than most women because of this death. Children living with grief either become steel or disappear within themselves. In my childhood, I did a little of both. The faith I obtained in later life opened me up. I am very much steel and I often disappear.

My Dad must have wondered as he lay dying what would happen to his baby girl. How would I learn about life? Who would protect me? Who would father me? The questions must have plagued him. The silence must have haunted him as the cancer devoured. Many of those questions would go unanswered for years. As a kid, I grabbed hold to the only lifeline I could, God.

God became the Helper, the unseen Father. My own Dad must have pleaded with Him in his dying days. Pleaded for more time. Pleaded for God to watch over me. God honored his request. I kept Him at arm's length for a time, but I relented.

I lived alone with my widowed mother for much of my young life. She is not an open person. She talks, but she withholds. Her expression of feelings is stunted. She feels, but those emotions are locked inside. I had to learn to read her. When I assess people today, I use those childhood lessons back with my Mom. My training in discernment began so early in life it's now second nature. I don't read minds, but I do read people.

Older people, hurt people, Black people, and especially women of my mother's generation were so guarded with what lay beneath. They found themselves leaping in treacherous territories where one false move, word, or emotion could get them flogged, raped, or, worse, hanged.

My Mom expressed herself subtly and masterfully. Only up close and personal was I able to stay attuned to what was lurking behind her maneuvers. She lived a strained survivor's two-step. That is two steps forward and three steps to the side—never behind, just close enough to appear on time.

Being so focused, I also had to learn over the decades how to tune out the noise of people. People manipulate. My own mother manipulates. She knows she can ask me anything and I can't say no. Well, I can, I just don't. I am a people pleaser. I am also a giver. There is nothing Mom could request or hint at that I wouldn't give to her. She asks in not so roundabout ways. She has done so much for me. There are not many things I wouldn't do or give. She's in her late nineties now and her time in this realm is limited. I am committed to give my Mom her roses while she's still here.

It's hard to imagine that if my Dad had lived to see 2024, he'd be 114 and my Mom 95. Their divergent generations, though separate, crafted rules that have been turned upside down. Dad would never understand transgenderism, men who are women and women who are men. He wouldn't get it, and I'm sure he would refuse to call a he or a she—they. He wouldn't be totally surprised that we have loads of Whites in our Black families and we all get along. He had a heart of welcome and love for a lot of people. White people would be no different to him. I think he would be surprised by the foreign inhabitants comprising so much of the American fabric. Well, maybe not. His heritage, I was told, comes from immigrants who took the name Bush. How disappointed he would be that remnants of racism remain. How sad that we have the highest political leaders in this century going back to George Wallace and the Klan days of his era. Separate but equal remains. Hearing lies about slavery would piss him off. He would find it crazy to think backward thinking is being revisited during the era of his grandchildren.

Some things within our own Black community would not surprise him. Our own internal skin color separations have not progressed as they should have. The haves and have-nots remain. Some prejudices remain against yellow and dark-skinned people. Yellow skinned folks are still favored.

The good news is we've had the first Black president, Black billionaires, and Black advancement. But some things have not yet changed. My parents in their lifetime heard Dr. King's dream, but I don't believe either of them will see the full fruits of its reality. For that matter, I am not confident I will see the dream realized in my lifetime.

The Lie of Fine

Both my parents lived in the cloud of saying everything was fine even when everything was not. From their perspective, all was fine enough if your family was not hungry, lynched, or homeless. The bar of fine was low. Survival was enough. "How are you?" was met with "Fine." As you have glimpsed in the thumbnail of my winepress, the aftermath, and my stunted start, I hope you will understand that some of my most ill-advised leaps were from a foundation of loss, repressed emotions, and the fortification of the lie of fine.

I learned to be fine when all was not well, to say I am fine and to appear fine. I was not hungry, lynched, or homeless. I was fine. For the outsider my world would remain fine. Let me repeat the lie—*I was fine*. But for anyone looking inside, asking how a small child losing their Dad is doing, my world was anything but fine. I was crumbling. I wasn't understanding how to just go on after my Dad's loss. Nobody talked about his death. They went on like the world didn't just swallow him up. I was upside down and nobody realized. I didn't have anyone looking on the inside. Nita was fine and that was the end of it. Case closed.

Upon recent reflection, I have seen that the "fine" DNA has tragically been passed down to my own children. Only when listening to my youngest telling everyone during her Dad's hospice that she was fine did I see the remnants of the lies of my own childhood. She wasn't fine! Her Dad lay dying in our downstairs living room! I was thankful when my sister-niece Tina pushed back. Tina, like me, understood nothing was fine about any of it. She took the time to look inside and help Faith. My youngest, often remarks how she really appreciated how her Aunt Tina talked to her during that time. Both Pam and Tina were fully there for us in our heartbreak.

I made efforts to talk and to look within my kids. I let them know it's okay not to be fine. I wanted them to be truthful about their feelings. I let them see me cry. I let them know I missed their Dad, that I was hurting, and I was not fine either. Not being fine and saying so was healthy and not weak.

My extended family still needs to learn to feel. We still traffic in the lie of our realities and the emotions that lie beneath. I encourage people putting on the pretense of *"fine"* to seek counseling. Today mental health is not a stigma. Don't avoid seeking help. I hope that in sharing my journey, my bumps, my unfortunate emotional lies, I can break the cycle of this lie called fine if not for my own family, maybe for yours.

Reflection of Relationships

The heart of relationships for me is bonding to another person, super-glue bonding where the forces of the storms of life don't break the seal. Togetherness requires mutual trust to expose real feelings.

Relationships, whether spiritual, romantic, friendships, or business, require a connection that is unyielding in the circumstances of life. You know what's real from the ones who walk away during your troubles.

I am kind to everyone, but I am not in relationship with everyone. There are people who are passing through and people who adhere to me. Hundreds of people have been in my life for a long time and thousands have passed through. It's hard to distinguish pass-through people from long-standing people because I'm not a clinger. My late husband, William, talked to people constantly. He would check in with family, old friends, you name it—constantly. That was not me. I love people, but there are too many and I have only so much bandwidth.

Many people have poured their hearts out to me with whom I may not have had a talk, a meet up, or a pulse check for a long time. When God puts them on my heart, I'm on it and my contact is timely. The pass-through people I rarely ever meet again. These people were not meant to stay.

For others, we bonded and were in each other's lives, making indelible imprints on our fabric and our makeup. These relations garnered connection and momentum for the purposes of God at hand. Then, like soldiers on a multi-scale battlefield, we got our training and had to deploy to other relationships. We had our time. Whenever our paths cross again, it's clear the reconnection was of God's making. We reconnect not from ground zero, but from where we need new sealing, new insights from the other.

Every person in my relationships I endeavor to treat with value and respect. Why am I telling you this? I am about to admit I don't have a lot of close friends. I have people in my life, but very few I open up to. I have a tiny inner circle. I don't often ugly cry for anyone, but God. I have my kids, my siblings, and people in my life who I am close with. People open up to me, but I don't always open up to them. People are in my path for a reason, for a time, and then we both move on. They may call me. I may call them. If I don't hear from them for years, I don't give it a thought. I think losing my Dad baked loss into my makeup in a way only other childhood grievers can understand. No one is here to stay, even friends.

I am going to tell you a not-so-well-kept secret. I have the gift of encouragement. People in the world of Christianity have some familiarity with that gift, but the secret is that the gift of encouragement is forged through pain. To encourage, you have to empathize with the suffering of others. To empathize, you have to know what pain and suffering feels like. I know what grief, poverty, loneliness, betrayal, heartache, self-doubt, and longing feels like. During this second round of grief, God added other emotions I hadn't fully understood until now (jealousy and envy).

Encouragers give a lot to people with no expectation of return. That's unnatural to selfish people. In order for me to get energy, I encourage, I teach, and I lead. My gifts build me as I build up others. The giving of myself is my energy and superpower. God has broken me over the course of our spiritual relationship. Why, may you ask? In order to spot the brokenhearted, you have to know brokenness. For those people passing through or the ones stuck with me, I ask the Lord to help me share His love, His truth, and His healing. Help me Holy Spirit share Jesus.

God has put many people in my life for His purpose, my growth, and their building. In opening up about my relationships, I am being transparent about feelings most people keep hidden. I don't know how long people will be in my life. I am unaware of the duration. I stay focused on building-helping until our paths part ways. Up until our separation, I am "*all-in*" until the boat docks. I have big smiles, laughter, and memories for the cast of characters in my roster—the talks, the dilemmas, the family, the connections, and the journey. I wouldn't trade these encounters and our bonding for any weight in gold. I love God's people.

LAUNCH PAD II:
THE GROWN-UP TABLE

Fuss and Animation

I've always felt I was older than most people. I have wanted to sit at the grown-ups' table because I was a kindred spirit. My perspective was lofty yet down to earth. I was nosey and quizzical. I wanted to hear what all the fuss and animation was about. Listening to their stories of days gone by and their banter that led to giggling and sipping was enchanting. Back in the day, older folks told kids to go play and get out of their hair. I love to see children curious about history and conversations. Listening is a lost art with our younger generations. They listen to garbage and not history. You learn more from listening than from running your mouth. That's a powerful life lesson.

I've encouraged my daughters both to listen and to tell me whatever is going on in their thinking, questioning and growth. I want to engage with them. In hearing their discussions, I can see their gaps. I can hear how they reason and rationalize what is happening around them. I'm not my kids' judge. I am their mother, their guide, and their unpaid at-will consultant. The stories of my leaps are as much for them as they are for you. I have tended to be the same kind of mother for my daughters as my own Mom was for me, but I dump in more frank communication with my women. I want them to feel. I don't want either of them to be two-faced with me or hold back what is happening on the inside. They know I'm not Teflon regardless of what people may think. I am opinionated and hard on them. They know I won't always agree with their decisions, but those decisions are theirs to make. I pray and want the best for them regardless of their own misguided leaps. Leaps are what life is about.

When it comes to animation of life, I believe everyone should experience jokes, memories, and laughter until their eyes start watering. That's the fun and love of family. Family knows your story and can level you in a way no other can (good or bad). My Mom didn't have a lot to laugh about. I doubt she fought to run to the grown-ups' table. I believe the grown-ups' table fell on her regardless of whether she wanted it to or not. Before my Dad, she was an unsupported, divorced mother of two young daughters with few options.

Take Care of Nita

After Dad died, Mom was more driven and focused than ever to survive and take care of me. Her first two daughters were grown and gone. They were mothers left on their own to survive themselves. Taking care of me was Mom's mission. Those were Dad's last words to her as we left his hospital room: "Take care of Nita."

She answered back, a little peeved, "I always take care of her!"

She didn't know those would be her last words to him and his last words to her before he left this realm. Looking back, I wish I had kissed him longer and held him tighter before saying, "Goodnight, Daddy," and walking out of his room for the last time.

Mom said years later she realized Dad didn't want me to come home and find him dead. She believed that was why he demanded she take him to the hospital that night.

Thinking about my Mom and me after my Dad's death, I can say I had the home life of an ancient. My Mom was almost twenty years older than most of my peers' parents. She wasn't going to every game, partying, exploring, traveling, or being fun. My Mom was surviving. To look at her no one would say she was old. She held her beauty well. For my Mom, there was work, home, and church. There was little laughter, fun, or play-time for her. She was ensuring she took care of me and taught me right from wrong. If she could get me through school, that would be more than she had done for herself or for my older sisters.

My home life was regimented: school, church, youth group, and visiting family. I watched a lot of TV to learn about life—*Good Times*, *That's My Momma*, *Tom and Jerry*, *The Flintstones*, *The Jetsons*, *The Brady Bunch*, and many others. Watching TV and eating were my escape from the dirt road.

My brother joked with me. "Anita, you've come a long way from the dirt road."

Yes, I suppose. Other than going to Leesburg for laundromat visits with Aunt Vi and Lillie there wasn't much going on. Aunt Vi and Mom were buddies. Aunt Vi was like my second Mom. They went everywhere together and had a habit of dressing alike. Lillie was my close cousin and like another sister. We vowed we'd never become twin anything. She and I were in the camp together with our single mothers. We loved each other, but, like them, we rarely said such words. It was a no-thrills camp for us. We found ourselves most times in the back seat of the car. We made the best of our lives. After Pam and Tina moved out of my house, Lillie and I were our own closest companions. Lillie was the athlete and I was the bookworm.

My Aunt Betty lived close by and we had another Cousin Sara who lived nearby. We weren't as close as Lillie and I were. This cousin had a Dad and we didn't. There was no sharing and we always knew what we were missing. We saw her Dad and we knew we could never see our own again.

Our lack of Dads and our working Moms were evident every morning before catching the bus. Her Dad made her egg sandwiches and drove her to the bus stop. We woke up alone. Our Moms were off to work by 5:00 a.m. If we were lucky, we could ride to the bus stop and smell freshly cooked fried eggs when we walked into their house. I don't like eggs, but they smell so good. Some days my cousin allowed us to catch a ride to the bus stop and some days she didn't. She had a Dad and we were Dad-less. She ruled. Monday through Friday we realized we weren't special.

If being Dad-less wasn't bad enough, I also was terrified on these mornings. Walking down to my cousin's house, I met their dog named Prince at the stairs. He terrorized me every time he saw me. He didn't want to eat Lillie, just me. I lived right next to him, so it wasn't like he didn't see me every day. *What gives, dumb dog?* To make matters worse, they got another dog, named Rover. The good news was that Rover was sweet. I liked Rover and he liked me. But Prince was another thing. I never wanted a dog dead before, but this little white devil took the cake. After the years finally wore on, that white demon spawn died. Can you believe he passed on his hate for me to my sweet Rover? Rover took over the job every week of trying to eat me! *What gives?* It must have been that damn demon dog's dying request: Eat the girl!

On a more serious note, I lived in warmth, ate good food, had godly direction, and had my Mom. Her being healthy and alive was the bottom line for me. Her living was my "enough." My newfound faith in God was changing me, but I wanted my Mom safe. After my Dad's death and before I knew God, I lived with the constant fear of losing her too.

I was secretly afraid of becoming an orphan, of having no one to take care of me. I had older siblings, but none of them was fully grown and stable. They all were barely living their own existence. I didn't believe any of them would step up. None of them really checked on me when Dad died. They may have said, "Hey, Nita, how are you doing?" I would reply, "Good." Then they would go about their business. That's not real help. That check-in did not cut it. I did get great health advice—wait for it.

"Nita, you might want to back off eating too many potato chips."

Really? Dad just died and your life advice is to eat fewer chips? Why would I believe I would have great support if Mom died?

In my mind, with Mom being an old forty-eight, she seemed ancient. I'm well beyond that age now, so I laugh at Little Nita. My brain as a child processed forty-eight the same as ninety-eight. For me, everything went through the prism of death. If Dad could die, so could Mom. Regular kids that see age, don't reason that way. From the day I heard the words "Daddy died," my prism was skewed. Even today I catch myself thinking with that same filter.

As a grown woman reflecting on that small child's view, I'm grateful God allowed me to see my Mom in her nineties. I'm glad my girls have had their grandmother into their adult lives. I feel like I'm in the movie *The Green Mile* where Tom Hanks gets touched and lives on. I prayed so hard for God to keep my Mom here for me. I think He touched her real good.

My daughters have seen only one side of their grandmom. They didn't see the strong Rosetta. She didn't have my Dad's fortitude, but she was her own force to be reckoned with. She used her physical strength to move heavy furniture around our house. She also used her mental strength to make ends meet. I didn't want for material things. I grew up well. I didn't know how tough finances were for her. I didn't know we were living below the poverty line. I saw only one side of a sideways story for a Black woman of her time. My girls see frail grandma and not the strength lost from her winepress.

I keep talking about my Mom because, in our development as women, our mothers influence so much of our fabric. From experience, I know my Mom struggles with outward affection (kissing, holding, embracing, or looking you in the eye and saying "I love you"). I'm not sure what the genesis of that is, but being one of fifteen siblings and an adult child of an alcoholic probably has something to do with it.

My love languages are physical touch and communication, the direct opposite of what I found in my upbringing and my home. I sought love. I didn't recognize how I was limiting my affection with my daughters as they grew older. I adopted my own Mom's behaviors when I was the mother of a teen. I didn't think affection was needed or wanted for that matter. Until my older daughter shared her feelings on the loss and absence of my affection, I truly was oblivious. I wondered what other mothering lapses I was clueless about. I didn't want that for them, but I mirrored what I had received. Had I fallen from having my mothering cape? I was disappointed in myself.

The death of my husband was turning on its head my identity as a former wife and now a not-so-great Mom. His death alone was a hard enough blow. Who knew what other bombshells awaited me? I didn't want to emulate my Mom's lie of fine or to be emotionally distant. Somehow, I had achieved a measure of both. *Damn.*

Sex and the Mailbox

Children don't try this at home. By the age of twelve, I developed a committed Christian relationship and did not want to have sex before I married. I didn't know a lot about sex but being the third and youngest daughter of four siblings, I had some idea. My two playmates were my two nieces one year my junior. In 1967, I appeared and in 1968, my mother had two granddaughters to care for from her teenage daughters.

How did my teenage sisters, Yvonne, and Clara, pull a fast one on my very experienced parents? Where my Mom preached modesty, chastity, and conservatism, my sisters heard fast, hot, and trickery. Here was their trick. They showed Mom acceptable school clothes in which to leave the house, only to change into Sexy Lexy gear for school. You guessed it—they hid their Mom-approved clothes in the mailbox. The mail carrier and my Mom were none the wiser until two bunnies died. (That's the old euphemism for pregnancy tests.)

My Mom had the double shock and humiliation of having both her teenage daughters pregnant four months apart. She had just given birth at thirty-seven and now two more babies were about to join the fun. She was a stay-at-home Mom during my infancy. One granddaughter was delivered 363 days after me, so Pam and I are the same age for two days. Tina came four months after. Hence the reference to my sister-nieces. They rib me for being older and call me Auntie when we meet new people. That was some helluva mailbox! It may not be obvious how my sisters' conundrum impacted my life. Well, it did—a lot. Had they not played games with the bunny rabbit, I would have been alone with no playmates. We all took my Dad's loss very hard.

Out of curiosity, I asked my Mom how my Dad reacted. She said his response was, "God dammit, two babies in the same year!" He just kept working for the family. She said she had a lot more to say to my sisters than he did. He understood what young boys do. He also knew nothing he said at that point would change the situation. My Mom, on the other hand, made it crystal clear that if my sisters were grown enough to drop their drawers, they were big enough to raise their own babies. It wasn't going to be her. She said telling my sisters they weren't going out of the house killed them more than anything. Mom talked tough, but my nieces were never far away from me in my early years.

My sisters weren't always around, and I don't know what they were up to. Whether Mom relaxed her standards, or they pulled the wool over her eyes, I don't know. This is an interesting part to the saga. My middle sister, Clara, was being taught by a young male teacher. Even though she was pregnant, he had real feelings for her. He confessed them to her. He was willing to marry her regardless of him not being her child's father. He quit his job in Virginia, married my sister, and gave his last name to her daughter, Pam. He relocated to North Carolina to start his life with her. Tragedy befell him shortly after they set up house, and he was killed in a horrific tractor trailer accident. This sent my Dad and my Mom down to North Carolina to retrieve my bewildered sister. She was barely a child herself and she was dealing with grief, a new baby, and the upside down of her life. Her new unseen mother-in-law was out in California. She had been none too thrilled about her son's decision. This was clear when the deceased's family never reached out to my sister or their new granddaughter over the years. My sister and my niece Pam held her late husband's name for decades.

I'm sorry for the tragedy but I cannot imagine my life without my sister-niece Pam. My other sister-niece, Tina, was the last piece of the triplet set. We were inseparable in our infancy. We were dressed alike and played like nothing else mattered in the world. Many things come with loss. Loss became a colliding force for the remnants of many of my family's legacies. Ironically, none of my immediate or extended family learned about the healthy process of grieving. Grieving was not a thing to be processed; we just learned to move on. This may explain the prevalence of addictions in our Black families.

Anita on Lockdown

As time went on, I wouldn't understand that my sisters' creative charade with the mailbox would put my own love life on cosmic lockdown. Me liking boys was of no consequence. As a teen, I had no access to boys. None. Nada! Dating was out of the question. I have always liked older boys, but Rosetta Bush saw all boys as sperm donors. All she could see was Anita and a third teenage pregnancy. She'd walked that plank one too many times before. Thanks a helluva lot, big sisters! My mother was my warden now. My spinach patch was safer than San Quentin. My Dad was gone and there was no way in hell his child she had vowed to take care of was getting pregnant. She got suckered twice but not thrice on her watch.

I did have a first boyfriend and a first kiss. He was my first and last. I squeaked in a boyfriend in eighth grade. All she knew was his name, and everything related to him other than telephone calls was a hard and loud NO! I wouldn't be asked out or kissed again until I was a junior in college. That was some drought! My first kissing experience was entirely too aggressive. My young boyfriend knew my Mom would allow me to attend a friend's birthday party. That would be the place. He didn't know that it was only a fluke that she said yes.

Those yesses were few and far between. I didn't know from my total lack of experience if my first kiss would be a regular kiss or a French kiss with tongue. My practice on my pillow and hand was all I could muster. Back then I had imagined there would be some level of work up and tenderness. Nope! With an overanxious teenage boy with hormones raging and friends circling, it was full throttle. I thought my tonsils could have exploded. I got the tongue down my throat. It was my boyfriend's all or none moment! Mission accomplished for us both. At least the skating rink was nice, but not much else. I got my first kiss and that was that. Future kissers were far better!

In truthfulness, I can't entirely fault my Mom for my drought. My evangelizing for Christ throughout the school corridors probably wasn't too hot with the boys. Between God, Mom, and my witnessing Jesus, I had a flaming sign on my forehead saying these panties were off limits. No mailbox was in my future.

I wasn't really focused on boy stuff in my early teens. I knew where Mom stood. As she began to loosen up and let me stay in town at my cousin's house after school, I started exploring school activities. I was involved in student government, the National Honor Society, drama, singing, basketball, cheerleading, homework, youth group, and church. I was off the dirt road!

The Love Affair That Never Was

Where I wasn't getting any action, believe it or not, Mom was. That's a little racier than I should make it, but she had a man. I can't speak about sex and my Mom, but a nice man came into her life. This was years after Dad died, but he came. In reality, there were two men, but only one who I actually saw show up. I would have loved to have seen my Mom find a man to love again. I didn't understand as a child the importance of a man in a woman's or a child's life. My Mom has shown me that cutting that part of you completely off is not healthy. I may get pushback for saying that, but I think companionship is important.

I saw my Mom happy with my Dad, but it was healthy for me to also see her happy after his death. This man confirmed that love after grief can happen, even if it's different. Like I said, my Mom was beautiful. I don't think my Dad would have wanted her to die along with him. I saw my Mom have the most fun without my Dad with this one man. He had money and he really liked my Mom. He took her on trips and took her bowling.

I didn't know what bowling in style was before him. He didn't just take her bowling—he bought her a new bowling ball, new shoes, supplies and they bowled. He took her to Vegas, Atlantic City, and places outside of our small world. I didn't know life with such excitement existed. I didn't know what living without worrying about money looked like. He owned a business and turned it over to his son. I didn't know Black people had that kind of wealth. I didn't know what love could look like after the death of a spouse. Even in my current season, I remember the lesson that joy is possible. For this totally unexpected season, my Mom had fun!

She laughed, she could be silly, and she relaxed. She showed a side of living I wish she could have enjoyed well into her elderly season and not for just a year. I feel like she saw a leap and she took the option off the table. She feared the change, the love, or the unknowns. Did she care too much what others would think? Was it me? Did she refuse to leap for a grander life based on the ghost and memory of my Dad? Did she believe new love was disloyalty?

I fear she cemented her heart to seal it rather than cherish it and move on to a different one. She taught me that refusing to leap and the "what ifs" are tragic and harmful. We will never know what kind of life she or I could have had with a man loving us both. She shared during my adult life that he asked her to marry him. Mom never told me that. She said she didn't want to relocate to Kansas. She believed the change and challenges on his plate were too much drama. He was a man of means. Fighting with his family about her motives for being with him was not what she wanted to sign up for. Mom was never about money. She'd lived her whole life without money.

Needless to say, we stayed put. She cemented herself to the house my Dad built. To this day she has never left. She has never had another relationship since that man. I find that tragic on so many levels. I think my Dad would have wanted more for her on that front.

Many women today have declared they are foregoing love for a lifetime. There's something lonely and unfortunate about closing yourself off to even the possibility. You can be fine by yourself, but don't put a cement wall around the idea that God may want you to be with another person in your lifetime.

You know where I stand. He that findeth a wife, findeth a good thing. Come find me, godly man. Our leaps are choices. I choose to love again and be loved again. If we take off the table every choice that frightens us, many of us would never learn to jump off the swing as kids. Leaps come with fear, but so does change. Water that never changes stagnates. I don't want to stagnate in my life. With every leap that has significance there will always be uncertainties and unknowns. My Mom walked away from love, and we'll never know what could have been.

TKO in Front of the Altar

I tolerate a lot from adults and kids, but three things I never tolerate—whining, hitting, and back talk. None of them fly with me. That's why you don't see me as a public school teacher. I would be inmate 77773. That's the influence again of my Mom and her generation. We learned early not to try Momma! I have told you so much seriousness; let me tell you a little levity. We lived in the woods and too much whining or, heaven forbid, back talk would get us an ass whooping. We might have to get our own switch off the tree in the front yard. We'd better not bring back a bad switch or Mom had to go get her own. She'd bring back a *branch*!

My family tells of an infamous tale about my oldest sister and Mom. As the story goes, Yvonne tried breaking bad with Mom out front of our little country church. By the time of the story, Yvonne was a young mother and was over eighteen. Maybe in her old age and possible lack of sleep she forgot the rules or thought she had somehow outgrown them. Well, in her mind that day, the rules didn't apply and Mom and her had a dust up. My sister spoke words in the wrong direction. Let me make a short story really short. My sis tried the ole' girl and legend has it Rosie Bush walked away as the victor! TKO in front of the altar. Mic drop! Mom 1, Sis 0. In preparation for this writing, I asked my Mom what the argument was about. In her nineties, Mom said she didn't know and that Yvonne was always trying her. Whatever it was, she went too far.

The Life of the Dearly Departed

Stories like the legend of my sister and mother have a way of keeping memories alive. In retrospect, my Mom didn't keep my Dad alive for me with stories about him. She hardly talked about him or brought up his name. We knew he existed but kept that reality quiet. I don't know if that was because of her pain or mine.

This scenario was so diametrically different than the stories my late husband told my daughters about their grandfather. The tales of Noble Helm Jr. are infamous and hilarious. To hear Rev, his siblings, and the Helm clan speak of Daddy Noble was so fun. I call him Daddy Noble because his family kept him alive in the largesse of the storytelling of his antics. There were many. This is in stark contrast to the crickets about my Dad. I wish I had my Daddy kept alive for me. I'm not angry or sad, though—I am sharing my reality.

This revelation reminds me I need to tell more stories about Rev to our girls. The memories are still raw, but when won't we have levels of rawness? We have to keep Rev alive. I will keep him alive; I promise.

Here's a leap lesson: The false choice of burying emotions to appear strong is a pit of quicksand. Emotions buried don't stay buried. They fester like rotting sores. Be honest with them, express them, and get help. Tell the stories. Feel the pain. Keep memories alive for the departed.

What Whole Looks Like

Before I got saved, outsiders believed my relationship with God was fine. I was baptized young, listened to, and sang Christian music, ushered at our local church, and respected my elders. All of that fit the profile and checked all the boxes. It was my own brother Aaron (aka Bush) who unraveled me on the inside. His new commitment to the Lord in 1979 exposed my spiritual charade. I realized after seeing his connection with Christ that I was acting the part. I was not genuine. My brother's openness about loving God and speaking out loud about Christ rocked me. It shifted my core. He opened my eyes to the insincerity of my heart and my lack of commitment. I was *cut*! The irony is he didn't even know what he was doing to me.

I was angry and disgusted with him. I was dealing with grief and this nagging on the inside that wouldn't go away. He came home during a college break with Christianity talk, his hymns, and his testimony. He had the audacity to stand in front of our little church and talk about Jesus. Who does that? I had heard fake testimonies all my life, but he was pouring his guts out about his transformation. He really pissed me off! I was mad because every kernel of his being was exposing my spiritual reality. I was missing what he had. I knew I was living broken and unfulfilled, but my brother's love for God was magnifying it. The bullhorn was so amplified I was sick of it and him. Even at eleven I knew I was incomplete. I thought my emptiness was about something completely different. I never in a million years thought I was missing God.

I didn't understand my soul was aching for connection with the missing heartbeat of Jesus Christ. No one explained Him in the way my brother was revealing Him. The void I rationalized with needing to be somewhere or want something, but never had I thought my longing was for God. I thought the void was about missing Dad, missing home, missing security, and being empty from all of it. How could I have known Christ would fill the emptiness? Up until then, the longing was for something I couldn't pinpoint. I didn't realize my anger with my brother and his relationship with God was the *point*! I needed to get connected with the God I only knew arm's length *of*. He wanted me *to know Him*. I was longing to be loved again. I didn't know by who and my *Who* was The Father, The Son, and The Holy Spirit. My double life of rejecting Jesus was over. I really did reject Jesus specifically. There was a time I embraced only the Father and refused Jesus and the Holy Spirit. I didn't believe I needed the supporting cast members. The Father was cool but forget the Son. I was ignorant.

You can't get to the Father unless you go through the Son. I needed Jesus. I wanted to be whole. Without Him that wasn't happening. The false life was coming to an end. No more was I going to be the goody two shoes girl—all cleaned up and headed straight to hell. The conversion didn't happen that cleanly. I recognized something was off, but it happened with Christ speaking to me first. One night after going to a Your House Bible study taught by Diana Lee, I went to bed like normal. A scripture was explained that night and then the question was asked: If you died tonight, would you be with Jesus? I didn't think much of it. I was asleep and I heard the words "Know Me." I immediately knew that voice wasn't mine and Who it was. I started crying. I mean really crying. I had this small plastic trash can next to my bed and my tears were falling into it making so much noise I thought my Mom and niece Pam were going to wake up.

I told Jesus Christ right then I wanted to know Him. I got up out of my bed and went to my Mom's room and bawled. She didn't know what was wrong. My niece, lying beside my Mom, woke up, and both of them were baffled. I just kept crying that I had to get to know Jesus.

My Mom asked in panic, "Was that Your House youth group doing this—was it a cult?"

She didn't know what was happening to her child. I hadn't bawled like that over Daddy dying. My arm's-length relationship with Jesus was over. If He walked into her room, I would have grabbed Him by the neck and never let go. I finally understood what was missing, what I was craving. All along it was the Holy Spirit drawing me. Letting Christ in that hole inside me changed my life.

I was not aching inside anymore. The emptiness was gone. I felt complete. Christ did that! Two simple words and my response to them did that. The Spirit of God penetrated every part of my small frame. My life was never to be the same again. I had never felt what I was experiencing inside any church. My experience was real. For the first time in my life, He was real to me. He poured into me. I felt my grief pouring out.

After some days I settled down. My Mom couldn't compute what had happened. Spiritual conversions were not the norm for the Baptist band. Baptists looked for emotions more on the Holiness church's side of the aisle.

She didn't understand what my brother and I had experienced. I was grateful to have the desperation and emptiness gone. My Mom was bewildered. She didn't question my grown brother professing his love for Christ at the little church, but this was something totally different. I was a kid.

Mom saw Bush with his all-in faith, but she hadn't expected it from me. I was a kid and so young. I had already been baptized and was working in the church. To her, I had already confessed Jesus, so what was this? What was happening? Why was I so committed now? Whatever she figured had happened, she realized I wasn't turning back.

I don't think she truly understood the vulnerabilities and aloneness both Bush and I had been feeling. She gave Bush the benefit of the doubt of not being crazy. Me, not so much. She relented upon realizing that YHI, my Christian youth group, wasn't a cult. She saw I was serious about evangelism. I was talking to relatives and people at school about their relationship with Christ. I was talking to older couples about their relationship with Christ and one another. I got purpose I hadn't had before.

I don't think my relationship with my Mom got worse because of my relationship with Christ. The relationship was different. That's odd to say, but it is the truth. I grew concerned—was my Mom saved? She was always devoted to the church, service, and giving, but I never saw passion for Christ. I didn't want her to think I was a nut job in my newfound faith. I leveled out so that she was okay with me and God. I couldn't shake my worry about whether my Mom and many of the church members were sleepwalking in their faith. Were they saved? It felt like they didn't get Him. It felt like everyone was just going to church to check a box. The experience was hollow and dispassionate.

I wasn't so off base. Years later, my Uncle Bernard, well into his sixties, accepted the Lord and left the church. He wanted the passion of Christ. When he found it, he couldn't stay unconnected in his worship. I was still a young kid and couldn't leave the church. My uncle had been a deacon at our church for more than twenty years. What a change in him after he got to know Christ. My fear for my Mom didn't wane. Where was her fire? I didn't know if my own mother's relationship with Christ was genuine and that scared me. It scared me a lot. What about Dad? Did he know Christ? Would I see him again? I found myself hinting to Mom. I would ask her about Matthew 7. I was basically saying no one wants to be surprised at meeting Christ and hear Him say, "Depart from Me. I never knew you." What did she think about that? Was she certain?

I didn't want a knock upside my head so that was as close to asking as I was going to get. I sincerely don't want anyone to find out the Lord doesn't know them and it's too late. Hell has no exit signs or do-overs. My becoming whole for the first time was the biggest and most long-lasting leap I ever made. My relationship with Christ gave me capacity and maturity to love others fully. My life, as you will see, hasn't always gone swimmingly or been sunny. Even in my dark days, He was there, even if I left Him outside the gate.

What's Happening in the Moment

Even with the Lord in my life, I was not an open book. Being raised by people who are private with their emotions impacted me. That foundational experience restrained me from being vulnerable in the ways that should come naturally in healthy self-expression. I have layers like many people brought up with these boundaries. I have shared with you about feelings and relationships, but something else requires repeating. I care about many people, but I'm not actually close with many. I can count on one hand the people to whom I would truly open myself up completely and feel safe, unjudged, and loved. One of them just died in 2021. I'm struggling trying not to withdraw. The remnants of hidden emotions surface when processing loss and grief. I find myself stowing away my emotions in the solitude of my prayer life or my thoughts. I am sure this revelation on being closed is ironic given I spend my life speaking and coaching others. I use my own stories to help others, so why not tell people my pain in real time so they can encourage me? Well the answer is partly distrust and pride. Again, I'm not keen on ugly crying or blowing snot in public. For this "Physician, heal thyself" moment, let me explain that no one likes to be judged. Least of all me.

Revealing my truth to others and here in print is opening up. I am doing what is healthy but not natural for me. To admit my truth is a good step. I share my weaknesses to God and you in order to elicit your prayers and support. I want to overcome this inclination to withhold my feelings. I make steps little by little to share how I feel. Writing *A Leap of Faith* has been a blessing for me. I have revisited pockets and closets of my life that I buried. For a time I thought retrieving hard memories would suffocate my present. I didn't realize that in not facing them I couldn't be free from them.

The craziest thing about being a presenter telling people my struggles in order to help them is that they still don't get that I'm just like them. I'm not perfect. I could say those words a thousand times to a million people. But I still hear, "Anita, I'm not like you." They say it as though they have failed to measure up. Did they hear me say I'm not perfect! Christ is the perfect One! Somehow the makeup, nice clothes, and proper English blinds people to the reality that *we are all just a work in progress.* Jesus Christ is the standard, *not me.* Being a Christian is a lifelong walk. The word sanctification is a huge word that describes our lifelong growth process. We run a race, but we walk it out daily. No perfect gift cards are given after the hymn of invitation. The relationship with Christ doesn't work that way. The Lord takes us through processes. Our growth work is not one size fits all. How He will grow me will not be the same as how He will grow you. How He will break and rebuild me will be totally different than how He will rebuild you. The Lord's deconstruction and reconstruction are private and unsuspecting. None of us want those embarrassing moments televised for public view. God has a front row seat to all our hidden moments. It's up to us if we want His help or His public outing of them.

People often refuse a relationship with Jesus Christ because of their sins. They want to clean up first. They don't understand that we can't clean up sin without Him. Our Holy God is in audience for every event (moment by moment) in our entire life, everywhere and all the time. Where can we be that He's *not* in audience? Check out Psalm 139. God deals with those of us confused, junked up, and unkept. That's me, that's you, and all of us.

When I accepted that I could be completely vulnerable and confused with Jesus, my life opened up. Christ knows everything about me, and He still loves me. When you figure that out, how good this trip called life will be. Without Him, there's a one-way trip to hell. My vulnerability cape is opening. It's a process. I started *closed*. I am not going to end that way.

The Walk in Amsterdam

At the age of sixteen, I was not well traveled. Mom and I had been on our own for some time and my brother married his high school sweetheart, Nancy. They were expecting their first child, Wesley. Because of the military, Mom's favorite son deployed to Germany. She was aching to see her Bush. Mom used her Visa card and booked us travel to Germany. Love knows no bound with Rosetta and her kids. At that age, my existence had been stateside and I was not very traveled within our borders. I found myself going from the dirt road to the wild streets of Amsterdam.

As strange as that may seem, let me share that I have walked miles up and down the dirt road. On those walks I have seen rocks, dirt, trees, snakes, deer, squirrels, frogs, bees, turtles, and everything in between. You get the picture—I had seen things on my walks. During our visit in Germany, things were typical, but the little trip over to Amsterdam was different.

Back home, I was learning about fast living, but not at this level. At the outset, nothing seemed racy to me in Europe. They ate, they had houses, fast cars, and the Autobahn, but I was adjusting. That was until the walk. I might as well have been from another planet. Bush and I had just finished running into each other on the bumper cars. Nancy was too far along in her pregnancy to ride and was watching from the sidelines. Mom wanted nothing of it. She wanted to enjoy her two kids playing. We are ten years apart and such scenes were few and far between.

We all started leisurely walking down the street. I felt excited and psyched that my big brother had played with me. Something directed my gaze to a window at the house down the street. I saw a White woman standing in the windowsill. That was strange. The woman was fully naked with her bush out and her breasts shaking. She was shouting at us. I was tripping! My brother and Nancy didn't react. My Mom smiled bashfully at me but wasn't fazed.

My conservative brother nonchalantly said, "They do that here. Prostitution is legal in Amsterdam."

We kept on walking and moved on to the next conversation as if that WTF moment wouldn't be a bell unrung in my head. It's a good thing I wasn't a horny, teenage boy. That was one for the record books for my bubble-wrapped existence. Another pleasant surprise was the coolness with which European countries viewed biracial relationships. Nancy is White. The reaction of her own mother to my brother being Black was a burst of tears. My brother said that until Nancy's parents were okay with their relationship, he wasn't going to pursue it. Ultimately, they relented and came to love him.

Her family was Christian. Racism is *not* part of Christ's makeup. They knew in their heart Bush was a godly, young man. It's sad that in this modern day, there are so many people who claim to be both Christian and racist. Racism in any form is not biblical. Overseas, in the 1980s, there was a refreshing "nothing to it" vibe regarding color barriers. There remains in certain corridors of the US a visceral disdain and stigma regarding biracial relationships. We should respect two people who love one another. One day, America, we'll get there.

LAUNCH PAD III:
PREPARATION BIG GIRL

Big Fish in a Little Pond

I find myself reflecting on the launch pad of college. I wish I had known so many things. I was not well informed about college life on an emotional, logistical, or academic level. My brother went to a military school and his experience provided me no insight on any of those elements. Our age difference and physical distance could have cultivated that lack of knowledge. I didn't ask and he didn't tell. No one else in our family had gone to college, so I was totally clueless. My Mom had packed Bush for military college. She made sure I had everything and anything. Thank God she didn't put my name in all my underwear like she had to do for him. I had all the linen, cleaning supplies, and clothes two people needed. We took multiple vehicles down for 300 square feet of space. My roommate came in and didn't think she'd have any place to lay her head. Can you say overkill? Nita was going to college!

I went to Bridgewater College, a small, private liberal arts school in Southern Virginia. Bridgewater was a school where less than 1 percent of students were Black. I got accepted and they found me scholarship money. We'll talk later on that front. Starting out as a wet-behind-the-ears freshman, I wanted to continue finding out who Anita was. What questions I hadn't asked myself I wanted to dig into. I had been a pretty good student, and I wasn't totally naïve.

My final years in high school exposed me to people drinking, doing drugs, having sex, and acting foolish. I had a little clue of what a fast life was, but I knew Bridgewater was far from it. I wanted to be a big fish in a little pond. Bridgewater was my pond. I didn't freak out because there weren't many Black people. In my first year, I found a handful of new Black girlfriends (Michelle aka Chelle, Angie, Denise, and Mai). I adjusted finding other friends to include my White roommate, Dana. She had lost her father too. I guess Bridgewater thought we'd have something in common. We were roommates for all four years.

Coming from a dirt road, I had high expectations. I challenged myself to experience anything and everything I wanted to do that I hadn't tried in Loudoun County. I was game for any and all school activities. I studied and tried things out, slowly but surely. I was a disc jockey and had a Christian pop show called *Rock Solid*. Bridgewater had horrible band-width for airwaves. I probably had two listeners per show, and I was one of them. That didn't matter to me. I was psyched to learn the mechanics of staging music, playing vinyls on two turntables, recording, preparing, and speaking into a microphone to keep things moving. It was fun. I got to DJ a couple of school events and people danced. They sweated. I even got someone to cover a slow song for me and I danced with a guy I liked. For a DJ, sweat and a full dance floor is all you look for. "Word Up" by

Cameo was always my go-to. Anita was pushing past her comfort zone. Good for me.

I was part of the Student Senate. Let me tell you about that unforeseen leap. One night in the cafeteria, I heard the crash of silverware hitting the floor. The cafeteria erupted in laughter! Near the salad bar, a humiliated high schooler was on her knees, frantically trying to pick up forks and knives. You could tell she was living in the hell of humiliation.

What girl wants to be seen in a server's uniform by older boys and have them laugh at her grabbing forks off the floor? Not one. I saw her humiliation and in one split second I ran to her side to help her pick up the mess. The room was still laughing and catcalling, and I told her to just go and not to worry about the idiots. They didn't matter.

That one selfless moment apparently started my political career at Bridgewater College. Some unknown person nominated me for student government. When they told me I was nominated for Student Senate, I didn't even know what they were talking about. That one act set me on the path to public speaking and advocacy. This is why I ultimately became student body president in my senior year, the first woman and first Black person to do so. Big fish.

My decision to help was not at all calculated. Empathy is in my DNA. I could never have sat by and let someone suffer as she was. I didn't think what I did mattered to anyone except her. I know how hard it is to be poor. That road is hard enough, and you don't need to be laughed at. That, my friend, was a bridge too far. Pardon the pun.

I didn't get picked on during my high school days for being from a poor family. Most people in my high school didn't have a clue where I lived or what I had or didn't have. Seeing I had a reduced lunch ticket should have told them everything. They didn't know we didn't have a lot. They only saw me as the singing cheerleader and the Jesus girl.

That high school girl on her knees was working because she had to make money. I held two to four jobs myself from my freshman year to my senior year to make ends meet. I knew what needing money looked like. I recognized poverty.

I was a poor kid attending a private school with rich kids. I was probably there so they could be exposed to how the other half lived. My friend Chelle said one of her new dorm mates was crying because her checking account was low. "Anita, she had $12,000 and was crying it was too low."

We laughed at the absurdity of it. Hell, we lived with widowed Mommas. Twelve thousand was a helluva a lot of money! Now that I think about it, my roommate and Chelle both lost their Dads. We all were raised by widowed mothers. Chelle's Dad died in the Vietnam War, and I don't know about my roommate's Dad. Bridgewater must have had a soft spot for child grievers.

At Bridgewater, you could always tell the rich kids who had Mommy and Daddy's bank account at their disposal. They partied all the time, acted entitled, and didn't respect anything that didn't require a corkscrew. They were probably parked at Bridgewater for the safety net or they were legacy kids. Bridgewater was supposed to be a dry campus. Rule breakers break rules. I hate the taste of beer and wine, so I was not enticed to break those rules.

I worked a lot of hours during the week to see eighty dollars a month. I was grateful for a meal plan that let me eat like a queen. People complained all the time about the college food. I was never hungry as a kid, and I was never hungry at Bridgewater. Some girl came to my room to complain that, in a local newspaper article, I said I was okay with the food. I was. She was pissed. She came into my room as I was lying down. She started smarting off and I just lay there. I was tired and she wasn't changing my mind. After she left, my roommate told me she wanted me to get up and tell her off. I had a lot on my plate and her complaint about food she wasn't grateful to eat wasn't worth the effort. I picked my battles and there were too many other fish to fry. I was eating three square meals a day. For me, I was eating like royalty at Bridgewater.

When I compare how I was raised and how they were raised, I could imagine that some of these kids talked back to their parents. Some of these crumb snatchers probably threw their plates on the floor. They probably screamed at their Moms to clean it up! My Mom took care of rich kids, so she probably saw a lot of things in rich houses. Those kids probably told their Moms to go to hell and their Moms said, "Oh, Johnny!" Johnny hell!

My Mom would have slapped my teeth *out*! I would be dead. This book would be named *May She Rest in Peace*. I recognized from the first step onto Bridgewater's campus that I was blessed. There was no other way that I could afford a private college as Anita from a dirt road. My poverty couldn't afford any of it. Thank you, Lord, for favor and financial aid.

I have to give a forever shout-out to Bridgewater's financial aid director, Vernon Fairchilds. When Mom and I took the campus visit, I loved the campus. We sat down for the final admissions presentation only to hear that the annual tuition was $8,000. They saved that information until the end of the tour. My Mom heard $8,000 and immediately hung her head. I could see the money was a showstopper. I didn't know our finances, but $8,000 sounded like a lot. Mom was scraping daily to find forty-two cents for my reduced lunch. There was no $8,000 growing on our dirt road trees. Those trees were just good for switches.

Mr. Fairchilds said, "Don't worry, Ms. Bush. I am going to get you all the help I can."

His words were reassuring. I believed him. I received the thickest package in the mail with my name on it. He was true to his word. I got full financial aid! Pell grants, scholarships, work study, you name it—this dirt road girl was going to college. I had work study and I'd have to work during the summer to cover the full amount. I was grateful to take all of the work on myself. I didn't want to burden Mom any further. As I said, I earned about eighty dollars a month. I kept about twenty of it and the rest I gave to the treasurer's office. All that mattered was that I got to go to college. I learned how to make twenty dollars stretch! May you rest in peace, Mr. Fairchilds. I'll always be grateful to you! The Lord had far-reaching plans for me, from the crash of silverware to the building of lives.

Happenstance

My college work study over those years kept me hopping. I was a librarian aide, tutor, special events waitress, and encyclopedia data entry clerk. For leisure, I sang at a local non-denominational Word church. I acted, swam, and was a play daughter of a wonderful White family named the Trissels. I had fun with my newfound friends and family. I stumbled into a routine and thrived at Bridgewater. During my exploration, I took an easy three-credit, three-week class during our winter interterm. I tried a speech interpretation class. It was a mix of editing, speaking, and correcting bad verbal habits. One class led to another, and I found out I loved speech, acting, and theater productions.

I enjoyed working behind the scenes, handling lighting, running from stage right to stage left, learning lines, staying in character, and hitting my marks. I loved all of it. I really loved being made up by makeup artists. During my exposure to the theater world, I loved learning the mechanics of public speaking. I had a great mentor who loved Gilbert and Sullivan. That's right the great Professor Ralph MacPhail himself. On the dirt road, we didn't know about Gilbert and Sullivan. I grew to have passion for the spoken word as I spent more time with Professor MacPhail. He drilled us, took videos of our speaking, and gave meticulous notes and pointers.

He gave us a million-dollar lesson on the art of communications that I have leveraged for a lifetime. I ended up minoring in speech and theatre. What a life-changing happenstance. I met up with the professor almost thirty years later during Faith's senior year at Bridgewater. I told him of my appreciation for all that he imparted, and that I had spoken of him over the years very fondly to my daughters. I credited most of my accomplishments to his training. I was incredibly blessed with people around the campus of Bridgewater.

As I think of nuggets of wisdom for those preparing for their educational leaps, I would say to launch with purpose. You may not know your true purpose in life but seek to learn who you are. Wholeheartedly leap high and long in the safety of college. Don't venture out into the deep with untrustworthy people or do stupid things that prove how foolish bad behavior is. Leap toward finding yourself. If you have an inkling of interest in music, take a music class. If an instrument fascinates you, take lessons. If you want to play a sport for fun, participate in a harmless intramural game. Get hurt, run, and jump, but explore. Find your path. Don't sleep through your life. I say all the time in my sessions you are the main character of your life, so write a magnificent script. I don't regret any of my explorations. I believe many of my experiences and leaps framed the Anita I have become.

My admonition about finding yourself should *not* lead you to believe the fallacy that you have to have everything figured out by the end of college. You won't unravel all of life's mysteries by graduation. You aren't bound by the paths forged at college. There will be many pivots. Rarely do all our decisions we make at twenty measure up to where we land at fifty. You aren't bound by some fairy tale or Lifetime movie to find the love of your life. I repeat don't believe the hype. Take your time with the marital leap! Most college graduates don't have a fully formed frontal lobe. Don't believe that at twenty-one you'll leap and land your lifetime career, life partner, and final friendships. That's not always true. People can leave college with lots of lingering things like addictions, mouths to feed, trauma and regrets. All yellow brick roads can turn if you try hard enough. My advice is don't sell out your own manuscript for your life story. Remember you are the main character.

Ten Minutes with My Younger Self

This is my magical wish for ten minutes of life advice with my younger self. The rule of engagement is I can't tell her big revelations. I can just give hints. Here's my quick message.

Hey Nita—it's me. I have limited time to tell you a lot of things, so pay attention. Hold tight to Christ like your life depends on it (because it does). Don't settle and devalue yourself. You don't always listen to good advice. Get up after you splat on your face. Not everything will work out as you planned but wait because God does make it work out in the end (the very end). Take care of your body, drink water, and exercise. Maintain a year of beautification like Esther (girl, does it pay off). Don't compare, complain, or compete.

Communicate what God has placed in your heart by speaking, writing, and living it. You'll see over time (nothing will be wasted). Love like there is no tomorrow for everyone you care about—one day they won't be there. Pain and grief hurt like hell—plow through and grow from them. You'll help a lot of people. Get support whenever you need it. Find your inner circle and foster it (start with Pam and Angie). Overcome failure with honesty and transparency. Focus on what's in your control—don't get stuck.

Some relationships will hurt you (badly), but always protect yourself first. Love and treasure the lives that come from your body. You get more than one.

In any new territory, establish where you are going. Why are you going there and what is your purpose? Set boundaries for your leaps. Know when enough is enough and move on. There are no exit signs in hell. Tell people.

In whatever leaps you make protect your mind, body, and soul. You're not losing your mind—just finding your purpose. You will love again. God won't lead you into a den of snakes and He won't let you stay in one either. God will make a way of escape from bad choices. You have to live through your consequences but hang on. Anita, forgive yourself and listen to that small, still voice. Settling costs. Don't settle. Pull us out of ditches. Run away from devils.

The Leap of Settling

God has allowed me to make some boneheaded, face-splattering mistakes in my life. The biggest ones come with lifelong consequences. I have to admit digging out from ill-advised decisions in romantic relationships is at the top of my mind. My first serious boyfriend, who became my first husband, was the leap that screwed me good. I panicked when it came to relationships. I had been in a relationship drought since the eighth grade. Nobody had expressed any romantic interest in me. Negative self-esteem issues were surfacing. What was wrong with me? Was I too chubby, too busty, too short, not pretty enough? What was it? When I found the first man with romantic interest in me, I ignored all the glaring red flags and jumped too far in the deep end. I believed I had to find true love and my happily ever after by graduation. I believed the fairy tales that I needed a Mrs. Degree. My time was running out. It was now or never. I don't know where I got such crazy life positions, but I had them. Let me back up and tell you how the derailment happened. It was the fairy tale "The Lie Masquerading as the Truth."

Anita Bush was her own worst enemy when I decided to marry Taz right out of college. I didn't consult God. I lied on God. I lied to myself. I lied to others. I settled. I refused to listen to my family and my friends. I refused to trust my mentors. I ignored every sign. I kept secrets. I bowed down to my immaturity. I succumbed to my demeaning self-doubts. I didn't believe I was worth the wait. I left God out. I walked a path away from *truth* and lived a lie.

This relationship started with a lie and my own people pleasing. In my junior year in college, my sister-nieces and cousins invited me over the college break to a club. Not wanting to be an old fogey and no fun, I agreed. The club had a twenty-one-year-old age limit. I was nineteen. A man came to our table and asked me, not my vivacious relatives, to dance. We danced and I was enjoying his company.

Out of the blue, he asked me, "Can I taste your lipstick?"

I said, "Yes." I really didn't have time to process the question in the noise.

I had just agreed to let a stranger kiss me. My family looked on the dance floor and I was kissing this strange guy. I didn't even think. He was a great kisser. I was in the throes of full lunacy and enjoying the moment. When my dance partner and I returned to the table, I had to confess I was only nineteen. He was twenty-six. He was surprised, we talked a bit and we exchanged numbers.

I reached out to this man, and a woman answered his phone. That should have been the end of that story. It wasn't. I was in a drought and living in a state of desperation and lunacy. What I'm going to describe is going to be brutal and I'm going to speak as much as I can on past pain. I met him again and he believed I was interested in a physical relationship. I wasn't and I was almost date raped to prove it. Unbelievably, we started dating. I was exclusive and I would learn he wasn't. During my final months of college, I experienced "courtship and infidelity," yet I allowed the relationship to continue. I was submerged in sick justifications and very low self-esteem. I can only conclude that the lack of attention from boys and my own self-doubts were behind my toleration of his disrespect and emotional turmoil.

Why didn't I just leave him? There were no excuses. I almost broke up when he proposed in front of my and his entire family. I felt trapped and said, "sure." What the hell, Anita? I caved. I justified he wasn't that bad. I let the demon of "he has potential" to set aside who he actually was.

He was damaged and I allowed my own remnants of brokenness to slam dunk my life. I was leaping into treacherous ground. I had no safety net.

I was distancing myself in my communication with God and everybody that mattered. I was keeping secrets. I was out of bounds, but I went down this road. I had my eyes wide open.

What I haven't told you yet is that I submitted myself to such compromise as foreplay and touching of private parts that should have only been allowed in marriage, I lost something. For months, I withheld my virginity, but during more and more compromising play I was pulling more clothes off. One time during our panties-on play, I realized I was entered. In an instant, I lost something so precious I could never get back.

I was shocked, invaded and betrayed all in one thrust. I was emotionally devastated! I voluntarily laid my body down for my own self-destruction. Yes, he took advantage. He knew I wanted to wait, but my compromise *ultimately allowed it*. I was damaged. I lost my gift. I lost myself. Something broke within me. Who was I now? What would I say to a future Christian man? I believed I was ruined. My purity was gone. I wasn't a virgin. I could not say I was a virtuous woman. I felt my price had slid from far above rubies to a cheap cubic zirconia knockoff.

I believed my compromise had derailed my marriage prospects forever. Who would want me? How could I now witness about saving yourself? I felt like a fraud. What had I done? What had he done to me? He, apologized and begged for forgiveness. He asked for forgiveness. I forgave him, but the wound was made. Long ago, I have forgiven this of him and me. Losing my virginity outside of marriage was one of the hardest landings of my young adult life. I was *crushed*. The internal wound impacted me for so long. I had emotional cuts all over. I was devastated and too ashamed to even talk to anyone.

That was the start of my double life. I had college friends and people in my life, but no one I could trust to tell the cheating, the sex, the destructive communications, and the peril. Friends and family saw and gave me unheeded caution. With the loss of my virginity, this guy had to become my husband. That was the only resolution to this catastrophe.

I didn't understand life. I didn't ask for guidance or wisdom. I made lifelong decisions in total stupidity. I was so wet behind the ears in life and relationships, but too arrogant to ask for help. I speak in the present the truths of my stupidity and pride so I can help girls, boys, women, and men not to make big leaps without wisdom.

Losing my virginity, contracting a sexually transmitted disease, and being in relationship with a serial cheater was less horrifying to me than telling another Christian man I was not a virgin. I was beating myself up pretty badly. I felt no different than a slut. I know now how absurd that thinking was, but I was over the top with trashing myself internally. I forgot about Christ's forgiveness, grace, and mercy. None of that was in my thinking. I believed I failed Christ. I knew better and I disobeyed. I listened to the whispers of shame and the enemy.

I wish I could take young Anita aside and hold her. Then I would pull her face to face and shout, "STOP THE MADNESS!" I would tell her to quit crying and walk away. I would give her perspective. I would tell her she is not a slut, but delusional. I would remind her about Christ's forgiveness and mercy. I seriously don't know if, in my young insanity, a visit from my older self would have deterred me or not.

Part of me was so far over the cliff of sanity there was no climbing back up. How could losing my virginity set me so far atilt? I can't explain it, but I was rocked. I made my virginity a god. I was out in the deep, treading water with no raft in sight.

Too Damaged to Retreat

As I went through this period before graduation, I was a platform singer of a praise and worship team for a large congregation. I was convicted weekly on my lack of purity. My double life was eating me up. I was guilt-ridden. I would ask for forgiveness but I didn't believe it. I would raise my arms to God knowing He knew my sin. He knew I had ignored His principles in this relationship. How could I sing His praises with guilt? I did sing but I listened to Satan's lies about me.

I sabotaged my life with my first sexual partner. To be fair, all of our relationship was not horrible. Our relationship had its ups and downs. He was a person that claimed Christ. We were intellectual, sexual, fun, and went to church together.

I settled for a man who had floating principles and no moral compass. I married the man his fraternity named Taz, for Tasmanian devil. His name was given because of his bizarre behavior during his fraternity indoctrination. This is who I saddled my life to. I knew he wasn't the best choice for a Christian partner. I settled on him. Taz had God as part of his life, but not the center. I saw a lot of his weird and dangerous behaviors before marriage. I still leaped. I reasoned I was strong enough to change him. How cliché. I didn't see the irony of his name. Satan must have laughed at God, telling Him that he named the guy devil and I still picked him. Satan can become an angel of light. Taz had little light and I still picked him. He was dark. God exposed every red flag that even the blind could have seen. I dismissed them all. I couldn't see anything past my lost virginity. I was determined, come hell or high water, to make this fiasco work. It did not!

For me, graduating college, getting married, and living with a dual personality was a lot in the first few months after I turned twenty.

My marriage started sweet. Our apartment was neat and decorated, and we loved each other. Taz had good intentions, but no foundation. I got passed little things like the kitchen full of roaches. I lived in the country, but we didn't have hidden roaches that came out in the dark. I had never even used a roach motel. I loved the city life of Arlington, VA. The neighborhood was alive.

About six months into the marriage, I came home and found Taz in the bathtub. He was soaking for an awful long time and acting weird. I asked what was up. It was like he was trying to soak himself clean. As I formulated the concept in my mind, I realized what he had done. He had cheated during the infancy of our marriage. The vows, the commitment, and I meant nothing. He had thrown us away before we even started. He was trying to clean himself, to wash the sin away with soap. He still didn't get God. Marriage doesn't fix what's broken about people. Girls and boys red flags get darker during marriage. His certainly did.

I should have known that and walked away after our first kiss. Our marriage had its flatlining moments. In marriage, I tackled the noose of God hates divorce. We talked. He spoke of regret and sorrow. I forgave and we moved past it. I can't tell you if we got counseling or how we moved past it, but we did. Most likely I convinced myself, I needed to forgive. I so rarely think of my first marriage that this writing about my early leap is dredging up old cobwebs long buried. I can say he stayed straight enough that we purchased our first house, a little $65,000 shack in Maryland. The house looked small but had potential. Beware of making big decisions on potential alone. If you are starting anything grand on "potential" alone -talk to God first about *purpose*.

The little house, the street and the neighborhood was nice enough. We didn't qualify for much. Little did I know I had hidden tenants requiring more roach motels. Both of us enjoyed building a home. We were smart, ambitious, and adventurous communicators. We both had great families. Being quick thinkers and talkers, we could sell an empty water bottle. We were getting along very well a couple years in. We created a new video business as a side hustle. It wasn't bringing in much money, but the experience was well worth it.

We were making strategic moves. We both got our real estate licenses. He would be the seller and I would handle paperwork. Years into the marriage, we didn't say, "Hey, let's have a baby." That only happens, it seems, in made-for-TV movies.

We were not trying to have a baby. We were not using birth control faithfully. We were having sex. I was young, and inconsistent birth control makes babies. I remember visiting my Mom and us having a romp one night. After we finished, all of a sudden, these bright lights came through the window. I thought the lights were from a car's headlights. I thought it strange someone was coming down the lane that late at night, but I didn't see a car. I didn't think anything more about it. A few weeks later, I realized I had missed my cycle and learned I was pregnant. I can't say for sure when Albani was conceived, but I think she's a dirt road baby.

The news of the pregnancy went viral. Nita was pregnant. Although it was unexpected, everyone, including us, was excited. We were headed to the big show now! My mother-in-law was especially excited about the pregnancy because she wanted a *girl*! She had three boys and wanted her girl, and I had the magic bunny in my tummy. Being a wife and a worker, and now bringing a baby into the picture didn't loosen the Superwoman cape strings around my neck. They *tightened*. You don't really feel the strings at the marrying or no-kid stage. Sorry, ladies, but that's the truth. As your belly grows, strings tighten.

Age doesn't make you arrive as a woman. Marriage doesn't make you arrive as a woman. Having a baby doesn't make you arrive as a woman. What does? Responsibilities and owning them push you closer to arriving as a woman. Thousands of irresponsible young and old females with babies haven't reached their rite of passage. Motherhood without owning the responsibility of bringing in life doesn't meet the rite of passage. Knowing and embracing responsibilities of motherhood does.

I had a pregnancy that was uneventful. We were blessed. I plan to tell you about motherhood and babies separately from this conversation. What I want you to know is that Taz started using crack cocaine unbeknownst to me during my pregnancy. I don't know the how or why's of that decision. I learned much later in life that he may have used drugs prior to our relationship. As you can imagine, during my first year of being a mother, I also lived through the full hell of having an addicted spouse. Without going into the gritty details of that darkness I will say I lived in spiritual, physical, and emotional terror with his demons.

Ultimately, I was able to grab our almost two-year-old daughter and flee for my life. I went back and forth to try to make it work—rehabs, new home, new scenery, new jobs, boundaries, tough love, you name it. If the monster doesn't want to leave the beast, there's little you can do. My life altering leap was known in eternity long ago, because Albani was born. God knows every life born to this world. Albani was fashioned before the foundations of the world. So God knew.

I can't blame my stupid choices on a dead father. Yes, having my Dad to lean on could have helped, but I had my brother to warn me of red flags. Bush warned me. I had friends, my sister-nieces, my play Mom, Pat, and my own Mom tell me there would be other men. I didn't listen. I was too deep. Before marriage and after, I was so over my head. I was so damaged I couldn't retreat. I wasn't listening to God or to anybody else with a pulse. This leap with Taz came close to destroying me, but thank God, it didn't.

That's how Satan conquers us—one insane decision at a time. I clearly jumped into a valley of snakes, but God delivered me in the end. I tolerated way too much. I compromised God's word too much. Coming out of a dead marriage and divorcing, I saw the mountain of consequences *pile up*! No one knew the horror I was facing behind closed doors with an unstable man. No one knew when his instability placed me and Albani in harm's way emotionally and physically. No one knew the infidelity, the secrets, the sickness, the addiction to crack, our financial collapse and the ongoing desperation.

There were incredible people during the journey of my marriage that could have helped had I let them in. I didn't let them. I learned the traps of thinking I was the "only one." Help was available if I would have only sought it. After my marriage crumbled, I left everything and everybody behind in that past life. That's not what the manual would say to do, but I ran for my life and I didn't turn back.

Had it not been for Albani, I can't say for sure if I would have left him. I hope I would have, but I don't know. The girl living that tragedy was broken. The good news is I did have Albani, and I did leave. My beautiful daughter deserved safety. In hindsight, Albani has had to live with fragments of my bad leap. God used that period to help Taz and me do one thing right, and that was birth Albani.

Calamity of Lies

I want to expose the trappings of lies and settling to those of you who think you are above them both. The reality is that none of us are above either. When you think you are, the reality of deceit will catch you unprepared. I got into that lie and made that ill-advised relational leap because I distrusted God. I didn't believe in His timing. I distrusted He would bring me a man to love. I believed God had forgotten me.

I compared myself to others, and I felt I was lacking. I wasn't. I should not have compared myself to other people, but I did! I compromised my values, my virtue, and my connection with God. I lied to God. I kept an arm's-length relationship with His wisdom, preferring my own judgment. I did the very opposite of everything instructed in Proverbs 3:5–7. I didn't trust. I fully leaned on my own understanding. On no path did I let God direct me. I learned the hard lesson about settling and sabotaging my life. Settling and believing lies are Satan's trap for a derailment. I derailed in my first marriage.

Admitting my flaws and realities to God happened in hindsight and not in the moment. God never cosigned my ungodly choices. My lies validated my stupid decisions. The Lord knew how He was going to make the bad choices part of His Divine plan, but I certainly did not.

This relationship produced a child God would use for His purpose, her promise and potential. Albani is a woman of God. She is already using her love for Christ to combat evil. She is tough and has a backbone of steel. I think she is destined for greatness. The hard landing and the brokenness of my first serious relationship yielded the great joy and treasure of my oldest daughter, but at a cost to us both. In my vanity and calamity, God gave me a gift far above the humiliation of my bad decision-making. I thank God for my daughter. She knows I love her and how God loved us both enough to bring Rev. Helm into our life. What a blessing!

My own mother's resilience and care helped me get out of the valley of my first marriage. I wanted my daughter to have a mother worthy of the legacy of Rosetta Bush. I wanted to be that resilient example for her. I hoped to be a capable and caring woman like my Mom. The Lord allowed me to wake up in the nick of time. He used the whisper of my Dad's last words to my Mom—Take care of Nita to wake me up. I finally awakened that *enough was enough*! Let me now share my flight back to the dirt road and the love of my ancient.

Love That Asks for Nothing

By now you have a full taste of my Mom and a little of me too. My Mom doesn't dole out a lot of advice. She demonstrates her counsel by her actions. She loves by actions and not by words. She asks for nothing. When I fled to her home, I was beat. I was broken and I had a baby in tow.

During my separation from my first husband, I lived in a cyclone. I left my first husband and my first house in another state. I was a first-time Mom. I came home with three dollars in my bank account. I had so much on my shoulders and heard the gurgling of my drowning ringing in my ears.

How did Ms. Student Body President fall so fast? I was in my twenties feeling like forty years worn. The only problem with feeling that worn was I didn't have any life experience to draw upon. I was a frazzled kid with age and no wisdom. I was grateful to be at home with Mom. Being around an ancient Mom made me feel safe. She had lived through storms. I needed to survive the chaos of my own making. I made the storm but was clueless how to survive it. I needed her to organize the mess. It didn't matter that I gave little notice I was dropping into her newly retired life. I made a phone call and told her I was coming home. She said she would see me when I got there. She didn't gush. She said what I needed to hear—come home.

Clara, Yvonne, and my Dad all made her battle tested. She didn't flinch at us invading her territory with laundry baskets and poorly packed stuff. Our arrival didn't appear to faze her. It was as if she grabbed some extra hamburger to feed the new tenants. I certainly was grateful. I was back at home. I was in the right place for me and Albani. I was with the right Mom for me to keep learning on the job.

Being back at home was a setback. I failed to launch properly. I needed a redo. I had to grab this lifeline before I drowned Albani and myself. I didn't realize how happy and relaxed I would be to be back on the dirt road. Albani loved being there. Between Mom, Aunt Vi, Aunt Betty, and a more relaxed Mom, she was spoiled rotten.

A safe and happy childhood was what I wanted for her. She deserved that. Grandma Bush and Aunts Vi and Betty had their little energetic bundle of joy to dote over while I went back and forth to work. I have so many reflective ironies in my story. I couldn't wait to leave the dirt road and here I had run back to it as my safe haven.

Everything was far from a bed of roses. My life was off kilter! *Full tilt!* I knew it, and so did God. I had left Him out of the biggest decision of my young life, and I could see the fruit from that choice. I repented and came back to God. He welcomed me with open arms. You would never know anything was off by my sweet little Albani. She was giggling with joy and happiness at our dirt road Disney! Out in the country, I'm sure we had some real little Mickeys and Minnies to play with!

Going back to my dirt road home meant more commute time and maneuvering than living close in Maryland. My job, my school, my church, my in-laws, and my network were over an hour away. Notice I didn't say anything about my friends. I had removed my friends from the equation. That's what addiction does—it isolates. Many things were fragmented in my life, but I was finally free to be truthful about my first husband's addiction. It was killing him and poisoning me. I couldn't trust him. The lies were the most sinister cut to anything we ever had together. I had to dig out of emotional and financial ruin all with the same prayerful shovel.

I had distanced myself from my friends and family in order to protect the lies. That sounds bizarre, but so was my life back then. I was hiding no differently than Adam and Eve after the fall. I'm sure people knew something was up, but no one knew about the drugs, the multiple rehabs, and the drug dealers demanding money we did not have. They didn't know about the multiple not-so-fresh starts for him and me.

I was juggling everything to keep up the appearance that I was fine and my life wasn't going down the drain. I told my first husband if the addition began to take Albani and me down the drain with him, I would leave him to save us. That's what happened. My motherly instincts saved us both. The snake of settling had destroyed me enough. Albani would not be the victim of my stupidity. I loved her too much.

Finish

My job presented me the opportunity to pay for graduate classes for an advanced degree. I worked for a joint military organization and a Black female Major named Pearl admonished me that I had to get a master's degree. She said my advancement demanded it. She told me about taking night classes and how military bases held classes from universities. I was leery of the Graduate Record Entrance (GRE) exam. I had flunked the GRE when attempting to get into graduate school to become a licensed psychologist. She said the colleges on military bases didn't require the GRE.

Here's another crazy irony. Before graduating from Bridgewater, I spent weeks on a psychology practicum as a teenage substance abuse counselor. Dealing with young addicts and con artists, observing them and their urine samples, counseling groups, and hearing their tired lies and excuses made me realize I didn't want to be a full-time counselor. Can you believe just ninety days before getting my diploma I realized I didn't want to hear people's problems eight hours a day? As a psychology major, I was a little late coming to that reality. Living with an addict confirmed that was not my calling.

I didn't think I was a daft person, but my life was unfolding like in the movie *Dumb and Dumber*. I was learning the difference between book sense and common sense. I was lite on both. As gung-ho as I was to take night classes while in Maryland and working full-time, I didn't know if I could swing this from my Mom's house. I was close to the end of my coursework, but the separation was pulling me to pieces. I didn't have much more to give.

I also didn't know how much more Mom could take. She was older, covering as my full-time caregiver, and handling all the household bills by herself. I was barely there and able to give her only fifty dollars every two weeks. I had to keep covering the expenses of the Maryland house. My finances were killing me. Digging out was slow and life draining. The addict was still creating debts to cover the drugs. I finally contacted institutions to tell them I would have nothing more to do with the loans they were giving him. They got the message when he wouldn't pay.

The big question looming was whether I should quit my master's degree pursuit. I was baked, fried, and shredded and there was no real light at the end of the tunnel. How could I impose and ask my retired mother to watch Albani during the day and most of the night? My classes were from 6:00 p.m. to 9:00 p.m. I wouldn't get home until 10:30 p.m. This ask was pushing it.

There had to be boundaries to motherhood. I was pushing up against them all. Mom more than fulfilled Dad's wish to take care of Nita. Years had passed. Dad didn't tell Mom to take care of Nita's grown ass and her little girl too. I'm being crude. That's the kind of self-talk you find yourself saying when your world is spinning. I wasn't talking kindly to myself, and my rule of speaking sugary got lost six months into matrimony. I was in the shitter!

Being a master reader of my Mom, I believe she had long ago learned to read me too. I truly don't know how the subject came up or if I even spoke the words out loud. My behaviors were showing outward signs that *quitting school* was my next step. At dinner one night Mom looked me in my eyes and said, "Nita, *finish* school. I've got Albani! You are too close to finishing to quit."

Wow—what a Mom. Just remembering this makes me cry. Mother of the decade! Her best-kept superpower was she brought peace and wisdom to most situations.

As relieved as I was to hear her words, in all honesty, I didn't know if I could keep up with everything. I didn't let anyone at work know I was separated, dealing with an addict, or juggling bowling balls over my head. I held a security clearance and I wanted to maintain my job. Another leap was I would eventually have to divulge my financial state when I divorced and declared Chapter 13 bankruptcy. I told security everything, and they were understanding. I learned I was not the only one struggling with addicted relatives and spouses.

For those who may want to know more about being a wife of an addict, I have to ask you to be patient. I truly just need more time to purge for this life session. A *Leap of Faith* has been cathartic for me. If the Lord allows, I'll venture back into that very dark place. I speak about those times in my speaking sessions, but I haven't written a detailed manuscript.

Pennies on the Sidewalk

As a woman of few means, I don't waste money on things my Mom would object to. Oprah and I share few things in common, but on being frugal at times I can relate to her. She once admitted during an interview that she balked at paying fifteen dollars for a hotel laundry service to clean each pair of her underwear. Even as a billionaire she thought that was too much. She admitted that she would rinse them out or buy new ones before paying that much money. I don't know if she feels the same way today, but I'd be hand-washing my underwear in the sink or looking for the nearest Walmart. I'm underwear frugal.

My experience with my Mom, my separation, and living on pennies keeps me in survival mode. Even now I don't totally waste money, and I never pass a penny on the sidewalk. My Mom made too many fine cuisines out of ketchup for me to pay someone fifteen bucks to wash my panties. Just saying!

Living without money changes you. My sister called me after seeing one of the book promotions, and she said, "Nita, remember us when you make your millions."

I laughed when I heard her say it. I don't let money run my life, but the offshoot of living without money is you never take it for granted. I am a giver, so I wouldn't forget my family or those in need. People always forget Uncle Sam will have his hand out first.

I am shrewd with money. My second husband, William Helm, wasn't raised with money either, but he loved to spend it. He hated that my entire family was money conscious to the point of being cheap. He would say if he heard the word "expensive" one more time, he would scream. He said my family and I had ruined our kids with that damn word. He also hated the word *budget*.

My family thought everything was too expensive. Don't get me wrong—if you see my jewelry, you know I do love expensive things. I just want to make sure I put first things first. You can relax and know my money woes and frugalness are not constant. I count the costs of most things beyond just dollars and cents. In my career I have to determine what is a need versus a want. Most things are never needed but strongly wanted. Whether investments, McDonald's, or job opportunities, I run a lightning-fast cost-benefit analysis. It may be five seconds or five days, but I understand the value of money. I am Rosetta's daughter.

With Rev's influence, our kids had a very relaxed spending philosopy. They would never break down a pound of hamburger to make it last for a month. Scrimping was my childhood default. My children have never had to really scrimp. In my childhood, hamburger in spaghetti was representative, not actually present. The Anita who found herself one time too many on the floor sorting quarters, dimes, and nickels will always have that rainy day fund somewhere around. I was not kidding when I said I don't pass by pennies on the street. I pick every one up and thank the Lord for my increase. I appreciate what I can and cannot afford each day. There's no running from the experience of poverty even when you have multiple bank accounts. I don't fear the what-ifs. I just have faith I can survive. That's been a process.

This is no surprise, that I come from a Black culture and an African people who struggled. We have a heritage of enslaved people and share-croppers. Our people can be both rich and severely poor. Money, greed, and inhumanity are realities that have left us with unseen scars. Whether a bellhop, billionaire, or author, we know at any given time, things can change. There but for the grace of God, any of us can be poor.

LAUNCH PAD IV:
THE FINE PRINT
OF WOMANHOOD

The Rite of Passage

Life gives each of us experiences far above what writers can describe in books, movies, or illustrations. Until you walk through your own valleys and feel your own heartbeats in your throat you won't understand how experiences and responsibilities for your children push you toward your womanhood. No one tells you being born with two X chromosomes gets you measured for a red cape with short strings. You learn in the varying stages of womanhood. The short, fuzzy strings get tighter with every unearned, unasked for responsibility. We learn that just being a human with a womb earns you a Superwoman's cape. The side effects of peeing while seated aren't properly labeled nor is the cape.

Women, here's the fine print on our Superwoman's cape that nobody reads:

Women trying to be strong, courageous, honest, and true: **bullshit alert** *– Women wearing cape in the face of anxiety, sickness, death, crisis, and disappointment are subject to massive tears, letdown, and endless weight gain. Child bearers wearing the cape can only achieve sustainable results when clicking their heels and saying the pain doesn't hurt five times in a row during contractions. Disclosure: The cape only works for fictional cartoon characters and not intended for real women. No refunds allowed.*

As women, from our first menstrual cycle and through our development, we wonder in the back of our minds if we are there yet. Where is there? When is there? It is the moment you know you can handle whatever comes at you. You've been around enough drama, mess, and circumstance to figure it out. As a female knowing you have the tools, you have the fortitude to bring life, guide life, and fully live life on your terms, come what may.

The womanhood rite of passage I believe is so different than manhood. Some men think when they get their pecker wet, they are a man. Far from it. I have met few men by my definition. I judge men by their wholeness in God, their masculinity, and their heart. That said, we women need men.

I couldn't tell you the moment, the day, or the year I finally felt like a fully grown woman. Even after having Albani and Faith, there were days I felt uncertain. I am close to sixty years old and there are days within my widowhood when I feel vulnerable like a college girl. The difference now is I know I can handle whatever comes. I am a woman. Vulnerability doesn't strip me of my womanhood. It signals, I need to remember my leap lessons.

The full-grown Anita doesn't rattle or ruffle so easily. Failing in my first marriage and eventually losing William Helm shook me. I lost my footing, my identity, and my assurance. I didn't lose my way or my womanhood. I knew Christ was the only way I could get through the valleys of my life. Valleys build character. My Psalm 23 valley experiences brought relevancy to who I was inside. *I am a woman who can be wounded!* More than that, I am God's daughter. God has sure footing. Whereas I'm teetering left and right, grasping for directions. As I walk through dark valleys of my own making, He walks sure-footed. He in His small still voice whispers directions. He knows the way. He loosens my superwoman strings.

He's been through the dark with me time and time again. He knows where the light is. I am the one who forgets. He *is* the light. He knows how to get to the other side and what awaits. I'm the bumbler in the dark. Only when I reach the fresh air on my face do I realize I can fully breathe. I look to Him and see that ill-fitting cape is thrown over His shoulder. That's where it belonged all along. I'm getting wiser to start asking Him for directions and having him hold the burden of my cape!

Delivery of Watermelons

No woman wants to give a play-by-play of her birthing experience. My daughters, like many young women, want to know what to expect. Here's the $24,000 answer: expect pain. Next question. The reality is all of us are designed by God to forget the trauma of birth pains. Read it; it's in the Bible. The amnesia is wise, because if we women had to remember the hellfire of the agony of those contractions, there would be far fewer little people on this planet. God lets us forget the pain in the moment our bundles of joy hit our chest. I didn't get to have either of my bundles touch me after their delivery. Black women and high mortality rates of us and our babies is a real thing! Me and my babies were in jeopardy each time. I believe on both occasions, had I not been a woman of color, I would not have had the experiences.

By now you know I have two grown women. My kids are about nine years apart. At this time, they are both without children, but one is asking how birthing was for me and what she should expect. The one hinting is married and at the thirty-plus stage. The other is unmarried, in her early twenties, and not thinking about marriage or babies. Because their birthing stories were as different as they are, I will tell you them separately. My girls are totally different except for they both look like me. I will try to share commonalities of the experience but just tell you the highlights. Here are the commonalities. I blew up like an inflatable balloon for both. My large breasts got volume for milk production. What goes up, must go down. What inflated like a watermelon gets compressed like a raisin.

Try as I did to moisturize and slather tons of skin ointment on my body, there is no hiding I have had children. Stretch marks and a very intimately hidden caesarean (C-section) incision malign my beautiful ebony body. Here's my journey with Albani, so buckle up.

Watermelon 1: Albani's Birth Story (1993)

Recalling the painful and joyous events of my first child's birth is not simple. Birth and the process of bringing forth life are painful, but when it's your first, you are not sure what's what. The books I read told me about theoretical things. You have this great birth plan, but no one shares that it's fiction, busy work. As a first-time mother, I didn't know what to expect with Albani's delivery. That lack of knowledge adds intensity to everything. I had read, looked at every birthing story, and prepared for the unexpected (at least I thought so). I had an uneventful pregnancy. I had no complications and I worked up until the day of her birth. I had a false alarm earlier in my workweek, but the delivery didn't start, so I went back to work. I lost my mucus plug that Wednesday. Contractions started that Friday night of that week. I remember feeling excited that the birth was close. I had been nesting and the house was ready. I was feeling the anticipation of finally seeing, touching, and holding the baby that for months was inside me.

I had been holding my baby within my body and in my heart, but we both were ready to meet face to face. My days back then started with me waking up and talking to her, and the last thing I did at night was to tell her I loved her before putting us both to bed. I already loved her, but enough suspense already. It was time for God, me, and the doctors to do our part and get her here. I am sharing female pronouns, but at the time we didn't know the sex of the baby. We wanted it to be a surprise. I'm shaking my head in hindsight because the safe delivery is all that matters.

Let's get back to the $24,000 answer of "expect pain." Prior to the actual delivery, I planned to tough out a natural birth. No drugs for Anita. I had been able to handle extreme pain, so I thought I could do this. When the contractions started, they felt like the worst menstrual cramps back when I was a teenager. I let the doctor know, and she said I was experiencing Braxton Hicks contractions. She wanted me to rest and relax. She did not know my history of extreme menstruation and clotting or appreciate the severity of my pain. After having birth, I realized my teenage menstrual cramps were the equivalence of labor. Can you imagine that happening to a teenager monthly?

Because of the velocity of the pains and their timing, Taz and I decided I needed to go to the hospital. Taz had just gotten home from clubbing and was tired. After arriving at the hospital, I went through another seven hours of natural labor with no drugs. Taz was no support, he was sleeping. I finally told the doctor that was enough—give me some drugs! She gave me an epidural. OMG—hallelujah, *Jesus*. I was so relieved, happy, and thankful. The next five hours were no cakewalk, but the pain was bearable. I went into the operating room to start my delivery phase.

I had the doctor there at the right end of me and she asked me to push. I initially pushed very weakly because of the way I was on my back. One of the nurses guided my hands on the bars next to me. I used to lift weights and have powerful legs. When the nurse gave me the grab bar, I was right back in the weight room, bearing down to push with all my might.

The doctor, seeing how weakly I bore down before, didn't anticipate that at her next signal for me to push, I would push like the Incredible Hulk, shooting out that 7-pound bundle like it was a 300-pound watermelon. She told me to push, and I put my strength into it. She turned for a second and before she could turn back, I bore down and pushed the baby out so fast she almost wasn't ready to catch her. My womb and my body felt instant relief.

The medical staff announced the baby was a girl. I heard the cry and relaxed to deliver the placenta and wait for Albani to be cleaned up and placed on my chest. A minute went by and I had no baby on my chest, no introduction. *What gives?* The nurse showed her to me for a second and popped her back over to her station. I didn't really get to see her before nurses started doing infant tests on her. *What? I'm the Mom. Isn't this my time? Don't I get first billing? I mean, what the hell is happening? I don't get to see my own baby. Nope.*

Apparently, there was an odor during her delivery. There was a concern about an infection. Either Albani was infected, or I was. Since they didn't know which, she was whisked off to the neonatal ICU and I was forbidden to have contact with her for the first forty-eight hours. *Are you freaking kidding me?* I had been with my baby for almost ten months and now I could not even meet her. This was *sugary crap*! God let me know from the start that Albani was His!

It was hard to imagine the first face she would see and the first voice she would hear was *not* mine. Her father was barely awake from the night of clubbing, and he got to see her. My mother-in-law came back to the room after going home to change and she got to see her. I got to tell her that she was the grandmother of a baby girl.

Oh, how she squealed in joy! She, like my mother, did not express many emotions, but that was not the case that day. She was thrilled with her first grandbaby. Albani's name was well thought out. She has my initials in her first name: Anita Lynn Bush (ALB). Her name was going to be spelled with a *y* at the end like Albany, New York; however, I went to the bathroom and Taz changed the *y* to an *i* so it would be more ethnic. I didn't know until I saw the paperwork. I was a little pissed not having any say in the matter. The name is unique and as an adult Albani loves her name. So it worked out in the end.

Trapped in the ward, I was bummed about having to wait to see my baby. I was benched and forbidden to have any contact. In the cosmic scheme of things, who does that? God, that's Who. I was right sided for whose kid she was from the start. Forty-eight hours felt like a decade. After the first twenty-four hours, there was talk about me being released the next day. I thought I would outsmart them and get up around 2:00 a.m. and sneak to the ICU to see her through the viewing glass or get in, but no luck.

My mother-in-law had center stage and an all-access pass to her granddaughter. No one was going to steal her first granddaughter. She was overjoyed to fawn over Albani by herself. No Anita in sight. She got to put on Albani's first outfit and style her hair. My mother-in-law did an incredible job. Albani's first baby pictures could have been in *JET* magazine. Nobody at work could believe how great her newborn pictures looked. Her lips looked like she had lip gloss, and her hair and outfit were perfectly coordinated. Thanks, grandma! My family was based out of Virginia, so the Maryland in-laws had a front row ticket for the opening round.

That lesson of being separated from Albani hurt. I had to leave the hospital without my baby. She was alive, but she wasn't in my arms. I didn't get the Kodak moment. I was experiencing a fun-less ride back to the house. How crappy on a massive scale this departure was. That was a lot. By the time we reached home, we got the news that my bloodwork showed I had a womb infection. I suspect from the mucus plug rupture earlier in the week. When it happened that week, my doctor said nothing about what losing the mucus plug meant for me or the baby's wellbeing. I was put on antibiotics. I wanted to nurse, but we couldn't even see each other, much less nurse. I was cleared in the nick of time. My father-in-law and I were enjoying burgers and I got engorged with breast milk as I was enjoying my French fries. I felt extraordinary pain, like I was about to die from the top down.

We immediately drove to the hospital, and I couldn't wait to get to Albani. I had to pump first and then work on her latching on. We connected well on that front, even though I did cry out in pain from my first latch on! That hurts! Meeting Albani was tense for the first minutes with Taz's father. My father-in-law said, looking over the crib, that if Albani hadn't had his son's nose, he wouldn't believe she was his son's baby. WTH?

Albani in her early infancy was very fair in her complexion. My first husband is dark-skinned and I am not. Bill Bush's side of the family is very light-skinned. My DNA test shows I am of 75 percent sub-Saharan African origin and 23 percent European origin. Our world is derived from a melting pot. My little Albani must have pulled more DNA from my Dad's side than was to my father-in-law's liking. He got over her complexion that darkened over time. He loved her to pieces like his wife. Thank God for her nose.

My bundle of joy was released the next day and we all went home safe and sound. I was grateful to have my first daughter. She was God's gift from the beginning.

Watermelon 2: Faith's Birth Story (2001)

To our complete surprise, another bunny died nine years later. I was with my second husband, William Helm. I was being treated for a food allergy only to realize in completing my registration forms for the doctor that I had missed my menstrual cycle. I wasn't suffering from a food allergy after all. I was pregnant! Rev was totally shocked and could not talk to me for two weeks. He did not think he could have children. I was a lot calmer and knew some things for the second go-round.

I was experienced, but I was also heavier than nine years prior. I believed all would be fine and just relaxed into it. Because of the weight and seeing how tall Rev was, I suspected the Helm babies grew big. This time, I didn't watch all the birthing videos. I had had a natural vaginal birth for baby one and I was confident I could push this one out too. I ignored any thoughts or preparations for anything but a vaginal birth.

I grew to be as big as a house. When I was five months pregnant with Albani, I had asked my Mom why I wasn't growing in my tummy. She said not to worry, my stomach would come. With Faith, there was never that concern because her legs were so long, they were under my rib cage and turning body parts all directions. My watermelon was heavy! At our first ultrasound, the doctor said we were having a girl. Rev and I sat in the parking lot and came up with her name in less than five minutes.

Rev wanted her to have Mrs. Fern Hughes's initials. Mrs. Hughes was a second mother and best friend to him. I thought of the letter *f* and we both said Faith. We laughed at how easy that was. Mrs. Hughes's middle name was Elizabeth. My grandmother's middle name was also Elizabeth. Everything was settled.

With the name out of the way, we were scheduled to head out of town for Rev to go on a speaking engagement. Pam wanted to gift us with decorating the nursery. We gave her the keys and when we got back, Pam had decorated the most beautiful nursery. The baby showers were happening, and Faith had all kinds of goodies. Her big sister when I was pregnant with her got five baby showers, including a maternity shower.

A maternity shower was a first for me. Faith was no different; we were blessed in every direction for her too.

All that was left was the delivery. I was confident and feeling great. I got gestational diabetes in the last two weeks and needed to back off sugar. Other than that, all was going well. We were given a due date, but Faith was running late. Her due date was pushed to September 11, 2001. My Mom's birthday was September 13 and our wedding anniversary was September 11.

September 11 came. I was resting in bed when Rev came into the room with a serious voice and told me to turn on the TV. I popped on the remote while in bed only to see people jumping from the Twin Towers. I was confused. Rev told me we were under a terrorist attack. I had never heard of something like this. I started rubbing my stomach and telling Faith to stay in there. I had been telling her to come out for the past few days, and now I was fully reversing course. I just repeated, "Not today, Sweetheart."

She didn't come as asked. Another week passed and we were all bewildered about 9/11. Rev's brother, stationed in Guam, called in concern. He didn't remember I no longer worked in the Pentagon. I had left a year earlier. Finally the days passed and Faith was overcooked and huge. She needed to come.

I had already decided to request an epidural once my feet hit the delivery floor. I wasn't going to be a suffering martyr this time. On Sunday, September 16, I started labor during a Sunday church service Rev was preaching in our home. He knew I had had the first stage of labor that morning. We'd decided to head to the hospital when he was finished preaching. God first. I was going through contractions and breathing through the service. Pam was there and keeping an eye on me. I didn't tell her I had already gotten the signal from my bloody show coming that morning. I just kept remembering the Genesis 3 scripture about childbirth being painful and normal.

During the service, the pain wasn't unbearable. Rev preached and concluded. He and Pam were hungry and wanted something to eat before going to the hospital. I wanted to handle the early labor at the house. They headed out to a restaurant. They figured by the time they got back I'd be ready for the hospital. Albani was eight years old and able to keep me company. That sounded like a good plan at the time.

I planned to involve Albani in her baby sister's birth story. I told her whenever I yelled at her to time me. I went upstairs and tried to chill. When the pain came, I yelled to Albani. So I wouldn't scare her, I went into my closet and endured the hardest pain in there. I still was trying to be chill and show I was a veteran. I figured there was no real rush; I could just breathe through the contractions as long as possible in my own house. The birth process can take hours.

My contractions were coming faster than expected and the memory of the birth pains was coming back too. My amnesia blocks broke. My head was remembering my saga with Albani in living color. Oh, the *pain*. I remembered all of it. I asked Albani how long it had been since the last time I yelled out. She said two minutes. I asked if, she was sure. The next contraction came soon after, and she yelled the time was one minute and something.

I screamed, "One minute?"

"Yeah, Mom."

I called Rev and Pam and said the contractions were coming less than two minutes apart.

They couldn't believe it. They had just left me a few minutes earlier. They hadn't even ordered. Labor was close. Pam and Rev opted for fast food and took me to the hospital. I was in pain. At the hospital, Pam was playing Momma bear and telling them to get me checked in! They were asking me all these questions and Pam asked if they needed to ask all those questions right then. Couldn't they see I was in a lot of pain? Go get 'em, Pam.

There would be no comfort to be had—room or no room. Faith was barreling down. Within an hour I was at nine sonameters. The word was out that I was at the hospital. Rev and I lived in Virginia, so my Virginia brigade was on the way. They weren't able to get to Maryland for Albani, but they were close enough to get to Faith's birth. I had an audience. That was strange. I was calm, but the baby wasn't progressing beyond the nine sonameters. I got my epidural and was just waiting it out. It took so long my guests decided to leave before the delivery. For my big day, I got the most junior nurse practitioner (NP) from my OB/GYN's practice. She was nice but inexperienced. There wasn't sufficient medical coverage for me and what was happening. She let the labor go on without progress for too long. The fetal heartbeat was not showing stress until it was almost too late. The heart rate was falling. The doctor was concerned and said to prep me for an emergency C-section.

In the wee hours of the morning, the doctor flew into the operating room and with no words just went to work. I didn't realize how serious things were until he went about the business of cutting me and getting her out. Apparently, the NP hadn't realized my hips were not wide enough to allow Faith's head to pass through. They should have done the

C-section much earlier. I couldn't believe I needed a C-section. I didn't pay attention to C-section videos or books. By the time I went into surgery, we were in crisis. He got me in there and cut me in record time. Faith was taken out, but before they could get her face fully out, she took her first breath within the sack. Her lungs filled not with fresh air but with meconium (newborn poop). She could not breathe.

I didn't know why my baby wasn't put on my chest again. Why was the nurse working on my baby? Why no crying? Why did they show me her for one second and whisk her off in a panic? Back then, babies with meconium aspiration had a 96 percent mortality rate. They had to get Rev. No APGAR test was administered. There seemed to be a full-blown panic. The respiratory specialist was working seriously on Faith. I could sense something was horribly wrong. She had a look like she could lose the baby right there in the OR. They worked on her and took her immediately to the ICU.

The ICU at the local hospital was not prepared for what Faith needed. Rev got the news the baby was born. He saw her in the ICU and took Albani home. After the delivery he did not understand how sick Faith was. We had turned off the ringer to the phone during the previous day's church service. When the doctors came into my room saying Faith had to be flown to another hospital that could perform heart and lung bypass, and I needed to consent. I said what? Huh? I needed to talk to Rev.

Rev was home getting Albani off to school, and I couldn't process the news that Faith had to be medivacked to another hospital. I had to choose between Charlottesville Hospital or Georgetown Hospital in DC. I picked DC. I kept ringing the house. I needed William. I was afraid. I was losing our baby before I even met her before I held her. He hadn't seen his child.

The hospital gave me forms to sign. There was no time to wait for a joint decision. Faith's life was at stake. I signed pages of authorization to allow people I didn't know to cut open Faith's heart and lungs. The medical staff was explaining and I was hearing English but processing full freak-out Greek. This was my baby's leap for life. Where was Rev? I was making life-and-death decisions by myself. What was happening? I was freaking the hell out!

Rev walked into the room after having no sleep and having barely eaten. He got both barrels from me. I lost it. I was talking too fast, inconsolable. I told him Faith had been flown to Georgetown and why. I could compute only that she was gone and I was not with her. I was freaking out. He yelled at me with such authority.

"Anita, you just had a baby named Faith. NOW HAVE SOME FAITH!"

The loudness and his words snapped me back into sanity. The words about faith settled me down. I grabbed hold to the God of my life and asked Him to take care of this miracle called Faith Elizabeth.

She was a full-fledged miracle because I was taking birth control, Rev had a low and slow sperm count, and I was traveling more than I was home when we conceived her. He was forty-three years old and just starting to see the impact of diabetes on his male anatomy. We had so many reasons why Faith was a God-given miracle. God wanted her here and Satan's trick to kill her and have me cave in to fear, terror, and hopelessness was not going to work. William's admonition in his strong, bass voice helped me regain my footing in the Lord.

Rev called Pam and the two of them went to see what was happening at Georgetown. I was stuck in a hospital on the sidelines recovering from a C-section. I was alone, frightened, vulnerable, fragile, helpless—not the emotions I wanted to have going into postpartum. The story of Faith's birth and her NICU time was traumatic. The doctor told Rev to prepare for the worst. She reiterated the mortality rate. Rev chimed back at her that the Lord told him Faith was going to be just fine. The doctor thought he was unenlightened and not understanding the gravity of the situation. Rev again said God had said she was going to be JUST FINE. At that exact time, Georgetown Hospital tried out a new nitric oxide treatment that worked incredibly well for Faith.

I was praying for her and pumping milk every three hours as if she was with me. I filled Georgetown's freezer with enough breast milk for five babies. Faith had a full recovery and took to my breast ten days later. We were two peas in a pod. I gained a sense of faith in that crisis like in no other time in my life. God has the final answer—not us, not our science. God is in charge.

Motherhood in Small Dosages

The most challenging part of motherhood was striking the right balance between being a good mother and juggling my other million roles. I know there aren't an actual million, but sometimes I felt like I was trying to balance more than one Anita could handle. When motherhood appears at your doorstep, you want to develop beautifully well-rounded human beings and not lose yourself in the process. Maintaining your own purpose is a feat.

My utmost legacy will be my children and grandchildren. The results of the foibles and successes of my motherhood will be on display for the world and me to see.

"Did you get it right?" That question will shine as a beacon of "are you kidding?" at every family reunion, party, and clambake. You should know, I've never met a Black person who invited me to a clambake. The bottom line is my kids' behavior will tell on me over the decades of my life. My future will outlive me in my daughters and their kids. I thrive on challenges, but this one was a little unfair and daunting. There are no one-size-fits-all books on babies, motherhood, or how to recover from all the screwups. That book hasn't been written. Who of us would have time to read it given all the jobs already on our plate?

Motherhood and its struggles can't be outlined in a handbook, a template, or a manuscript. Even our mothers say very little and then offer help in small dosages. The dosages are so tiny they don't give you the blueprint you need to figure out what the hell you are doing with these tiny creatures. Our experienced mothers give you just enough moral support so you don't pack your bags and drop the kid off after delivery.

In fairness to my Mom, I suspect with all the kids, grandkids, and greats she raised, she was tired. She did pretty well when looking after her litter. My Mom realized with her own mother handling fifteen kids, an alcoholic husband, and scores of grandkids finding their way into her two-bedroom house, that her Nita would figure things out. She knew every woman learns motherhood by trial and error. I would be no different. I had much better circumstances than she did. It was a safe bet since most infants dying weren't dying from incompetent mothering. She was confident that I'd be fine with Albani and Faith. Motherhood's challenges are complete on-the-job training.

Here's some levity. Kids are the greatest excuses for hosting great parties. As mothers, we get to plan the parties we wished we had as kids. I sure planned some great fun for the kids when they were little. I was the party Momma for our neighborhood. Every kid was welcomed and I had plenty of food, fun, and music for Moms, Dads, kids, and the wandering sales guy. I was totally exhausted with my parties, but they were off the chart. Rev cut me off after my last big party when Faith was two. I did have everybody in our house and backyard. It's a wonder the newspapers didn't cover it.

Raising Look-Alikes Ain't Easy

When you realize that as a grown-up, you are building and nurturing yourself along successfully with your mini-me (one kid at a time), you decompress a little. Caution: all kids are not alike. When girls hit puberty, they become two-legged piranhas. Hormones battling hormones is not pretty.

If you can store up a bag full of humor and grease to let things roll off your back, you can sustain living with teenagers. I got caught without the bag of humor or the jar of grease on some occasions, but both my lionesses lived. As mothers, we remember our little bundles when all they needed was a filled sippy cup of their favorite juice and a baggie of Cheerios. How did these lovely sweetie pies grow fangs at the mention of something they think is outdated and absurd?

My kids knew they could go so far and not too much farther. I don't deal with smart-aleck kids who backtalk and hit. They could buck but so much and speak up with a level of boldness. They knew the precision had to be decibels right because if I said to watch their tone, it was teetering on an ass whooping for breaking the commands of the king or queen of the house.

We all seek to perform the huge task of motherhood well. During the performance, we are making decisions in the face of emotions. All of us are learning motherhood on the job. Some of our lessons will be embraced and others will fall off the truck, never to be picked up again. During my first attempts with my older one, I was totally green. As I went through the repeat performance with my younger one, she was different and so was I.

Both of my women have become more appreciative of their master copy and understand I gave them my best. I was not always right and not always wrong, but my attempts at motherhood were always made in love. History is not shortsighted, but the reality of making decisions is very judgy and uncertain. It's okay to question if we are doing motherhood right; just know there are no absolute right answers. If that was the gauge, none of us would be allowed to deliver our watermelons. Anita's A game or C game always proved up to the task.

Kids Copy the Darndest Things

My kids grab the craziest traits from us. Rev as my kids' father and me as their mother was a peculiar combination. We were joined at the hip on most things, but not all. Rev is from a Midwestern family of five kids and divorced parents. I came from an unlikely pairing and didn't have a lot of exposure to how a two-person household works.

My husband was a Christian pastor, and you would figure we'd be super religious and raised preacher's kids (PKs). Our household was regular and not religious at all. We talked, laughed, farted, watched TV, ate pizza, and heard the latest R&B and hip-hop jams like many

Black families. Many people didn't know Rev loved music. He wished he'd never picked up a football, but an instrument instead. Here are the strangest traits our kids copied.

For me, tuna casserole must be paired with applesauce. One kid was cool with that whereas the other believed, like her Dad, that tuna casserole can be eaten only with potato chips. One kid loves everything with ketchup like me and the other doesn't need ketchup, but whatever she eats needs to be clumped together. She claims to get that from me, but I think it looks gross. No way she got that from me. Both kids can be organized, but neither kid got the DNA from their dad to clean up rooms and houses. I have clean up DNA but not like Rev. Yes, if there is an event, they can do the deed, but as the norm, the rooms they live in are not ready for a military-style inspection.

Both of our girls copied some level of empathy, helpfulness, and serving. They grew muscles in this area. They emulated these traits enough that the muscles strengthened. I don't know if I exhibited sufficient active listening skills within the family walls. Both Rev and I as parents gave full attention to those outside our house walls, and we sometimes discounted our own children. When you listen to society, church members and constant 24/7 phone calls, you want quiet behind the walls of your home. Our kids suffered from not always having the best communicators when they needed it.

We did a lot of talking, but there were times our children got the short end of the stick. They got the low meter of our bandwidth. During my husband's illness, the girls definitely got the short end of the stick. That is no excuse, but the reality of our existence. Our youngest bore the brunt of copying me as the caregiver. I was called the nurse-wife at the hospital. My girls have the capacity to copy this nurse-wife characteristic.

My tribe has copied the lesson of working together for a common cause. They operate in forgiveness. I know with our family we exercised quick forgiveness. When we lived on the island of a preacher's family, our kids only really had each other, so they learned to sulk and get over it before the next night.

I end with telling you silly things my kids copied from us. I am frugal and I shop at thrift stores, consignments, estate sales, and yard hustles. Both kids can shop high-end stores or at the bottom of a thrift barrel. What they copied from their Dad is that they say what they want to say with full fury. The "tell it like it is"—that's all Rev. I'm the politician. Rev will shoot you his opinion with both barrels. Depending on the situation, both of our girls can be straight and controlling. They get the controlling part from me. They know how to speak with two voices. They will speak with their mother's professional voice for work and switch over to slang with their friends.

Here is a running list of the nice characteristics they copied for the benefit of society:

They like to be kind. They love fun and being chill. They don't put on airs or act entitled. They love good food and eating well. They love traveling with treats and plenty of good sandwiches. They have great endurance for long rides.

Both are full of empathy for older people. They have great organization and adaptability skills. Innovation is their middle names. They love the Lord and seek to minister. They both will take on battles that must be fought. They know the value of "thank you" and caring for one another. They are driven to hear "well done" in heaven one day. The trait Rev and I most valued about them both is they are kind and generous people.

The Haste of Life

In talking about the haste of my life journey, can I plead the Fifth? I move like a freight train when it comes to living. I don't believe we are working with a lot of time. We have today and the rest is a guess. I live by that premise. Tomorrow is not a given. Get done what you need to do today. I can try to fill a twenty-four-hour cycle with a lot of complex tasks that some might say would take a couple of weeks. If I think of a task and a result, I want to see both materialize. As an example, my poor Faith knows with this manuscript, I have had little patience for the other pieces beyond the manuscript. If she mentions pictures, the cover and marketing I get overwhelmed with trying to multi-task. If I recognize the tasks, I'll start working them.

I'm a Christian, so I live knowing God is first in my life. I thrive on my words, my work, purpose, and all of them together can be a double-edged sword. My life can be complex and messy. I have to be careful always moving in haste. Jesus was never in a hurry and He was the Savior of the world. I have to watch being Madame Know It All, Do It All and Be It All. Those titles don't serve me well. God can do everything and not Nita!

I try to listen to others and let them try things their way. I have found that when you are part of the 80/20 in the Christian kingdom, many people figure out ways to make excuses to get out of work. I'm used to planning and executing by myself. When I see a lot of people make excuses for what I have done alone, it bugs me. Sometimes I rather take on projects alone than work by committee. That is the foundation of me multi-tasking and moving like a freight train.

As I reflect on haste, I am often reminded that rushing can be a sin. Jesus never was in a rush for anything. He recognized the timing of God.

I am still a work in progress on waiting on the timing of God. As I reflect on my last seasons of life, I seek more direction from the real know it all—God. *What do you want me to do? Where do you want me to go? How do you want me to move in your Spirit?* I get more done without haste. My gallop slows as he prunes me. Pruning hurts, but I know He's doing it so I can slow down and bear more fruit.

For the eighty percenters on the sidelines, haste and urgency may not register. They may watch so much that they miss haste while they are distracted by the popcorn as the credits roll. When you are in the ring doing the work of the Lord, you don't stop to ask for the soda-popcorn combo. So with the haste of life, I'm moving. I will continue to press toward the mark as long as the Lord breathes the breath of life into my lungs each day. Praise God for the breath!

The Circle of Friendship

I would be remiss to end this launch pad without revealing the fortress of my womanhood—friendships. I have a handful of friends who hold me up. My best friend is God, followed by my late husband, William. I was greatly blessed to meet some incredible men and women who have held down the woman with the bright smile, head of hair, and mouth almighty. I am not a woman who can do everything on my own. I haven't!

Whether it takes a village or the secret society of the sisterhood of the traveling pants, the fact remains I have always needed help. I couldn't have survived this far without support. When I went through the isolation of addiction with my first husband, I learned the hard way that I need a village. I tried to survive in secrecy and I almost crumbled. I couldn't survive the strangling of the cape around my neck. New Christian men and women that God allowed in my life came in the nick of time. I was never suicidal, but I was low. He loosened the strings, but He allowed others to strengthen me in friendship and compassion. Sometimes, just a kind word of understanding is all a suffering soul needs.

My new friends and Christian family members saw the wounds of the strings and walked with me as I came through restoration. The journey back to health was not quick. Rev specifically was loving and kind to me in friendship. We did not start out as anything but fellow Christians. Our relationship changed long after our friendship had solidified. That friendship turned to love.

As an illustration of me and how I view friendship three dimensionally, I would like to offer up one of my favorite movies, *Steel Magnolias*. The movie describes friendship and at the same time embodies my dimensions. That may surprise some of you because the movie is made up of an almost all-White female cast. It's not their outward appearance that reflects me, but the compilation of strong, frail, and flawed women. They collectively emulate Anita through and through.

Here is the cast list of the 1989 movie *Steel Magnolias* and why I say they show you a peek of me. Let's start with Sally Field (M'Lynn Eatenton). She was smart, fierce for her family, the rock, the caregiver, the pusher, the brokenhearted, the persevering woman, Mom, wife, and friend. Remind you of anyone? Let's take Julia Roberts (Shelby Eatenton). She was married not so happily. She became sick, needed a kidney, and had a child hoping to help the marriage, only to sacrifice her life. She was a nurse who ignored what she should have known. No, Anita did not have a baby hoping to save a marriage, but I was a psychology major who should have known a person was unbalanced and unhealthy.

We cannot forget Shirley MacLaine (Ouiser Boudre). What a character. She was wealthy, widowed, and on the outside tough, but she was caring and would die for her friends. Then there's Dolly Parton (Truvy Jones). She was a businesswoman, married, a sweetheart, kind, giving, and she and her husband loved one another, but she inwardly wanted more. With the death of Shelby, her husband realized just how special she was and decided to treasure their love and demonstrated that love by surprising her with a second salon. He loved and believed in her dreams. Ironically, all through middle school I was bullied, called Dolly Junior or Stuff and Puff. Two idiot girls thought I stuffed toilet paper to generate my 36D breast size. Nothing was stuffed in my shirt!

We can't overlook one of my favorite women, Olympia Dukakis (Clairee Belcher). She was wealthy, stylish, sophisticated, witty, and hilarious. Clairee had a smile that beamed in any room or situation. She could lighten the tensest moments with just the right zingers. She was real. I have often said Clairee's catch phrase to both of my girls: "I love you more than my luggage." (That's a line from Clairee to Ouiser at the cemetery where Ouiser tells her to get off her bench!) This character, as sophisticated as she was, had the ability to read a room. That's me through and through. I don't read minds, but I can read a room.

The last character of this ensemble was a very young woman. Daryl Hannah's (Annelle Dupuy) character who was finding her way in life, her faith, and a new environment. She wanted to please God and fit in. She stumbled upon these older seasoned women like a curious little girl. Her heart was pure, but she was too uptight and wanted Jesus in her heart without letting loose or being sinful. I could identify with the confusion and how Annelle loved the Lord but had to find the balance between religion and her view of legalism and the liberty and freedom of a faith relationship with Jesus.

The two halves of the religious world haven't come to a meeting of the minds on that disconnect. Jesus was never legalistic. That's something we made up. Annelle navigated loving her boyfriend, who eventually became her husband after some fire and desire battles. Their scenes in the movie, like in life, were funny to me. He loved this great-looking girl all covered up within her conservatism. He was as in love with her as he was confused by her. He was just trying to figure her out. Along the way he must have grown to love her Lord somehow and someway. Life has a way of working together all of our leaps. Some leaps end in soft landings and others are butt-hurting. Either way, they foreshadow our life filled with confusion, pain, awkwardness, and delights. That's life. That's ultimately why we all need a circle of great friends to laugh, cry, and walk with along the way.

My Midwestern Prince

I was incredibly fortunate to find friends during a confusing season of my life. After my leap of settling, moving from Maryland to Virginia, and starting over, I gained a great friend and brother. William Dallas Helm and I, like my own mother and father, were an unlikely pairing. He was my senior by nine years. I was as inexperienced and tight as he was a world traveler and open. Our colliding in one another's life produced a beautiful child named Faith. He became both my daughters' father. Thank You, Lord.

Only God could have brought Rev and me together in the space and time we met. We often said if we had met as kids, his age would have made our coupling illegal. If we had met midstream, we had other lessons to learn. We had to meet at that appointed time or we could never be together. We were great friends before we became great lovers. Besides my salvation leap, this was the most amazing and joyful leap of my life. I became William Helm's best friend and wife. I am grateful for God's divine hand in our union. The growth of my personhood and my makeup as a woman, a mother, and a servant of the Most High God is credited to William. Most people heard me call him Rev, but during our private moments, I called him William.

I actually loved calling him Rev more than William. Albani and I in our early years got used to calling him Rev. Helm. I just shortened it. Most people in churches and his Orlando Crew friends would call him a combination of Rev, Pastor, Doc, 'Preacha', Bill or Helm. Between RBC, the Orlando Crew, Blenn, the Decatur connection, Hudson, the Helm clan, and a host of people, I could always tell who was calling just by how they addressed him. I loved my big ole bowling ball head Decatur, Illinois boy. He was my big giant and a cuddly teddy bear. My man could roar like a lion and turn and be as gentle as a dove. I could write volumes for how he cared for me and Albani in those initial years.

He spoiled our little Albani. She was the child he always wanted and God let him have. We would have been content with just her. I wanted a child with William, but he didn't think he could physically have children based on his past marriage. He was concerned for how my family would accept his child. There were initial schisms in our relationship with my family. The thought of anyone bullying or hurting his child because of him might send him to jail.

God knew differently. Faith was our miracle baby in many ways, not just her delivery horrors. I became pregnant while taking the pill. Rev had questionable swimmers, and I was gone most of the week on travel.

God made lightning in a bottle. Faith is here and she is so loved by all our families. Rev's fears were never realized. I could sing lullabies for how he cherished and spoiled Albani and Faith. William loved his kids. I miss him all the time. I could not thank God enough for allowing me to have such a love. Boy, he and I loved to talk. My talking buddy was an Olympic gold medalist. Anyone who would call, would know he could talk for hours about the Lord and the Bible. He was one of a kind. He knew when he died, I would miss our communication the most. We had great times in travel, in fellowship, in kinship, in friendship, and in our life together.

The leap of my failed first marriage relationship was overshadowed by the great joys of my twenty-five years with William. I know technically I have had two marriages, but I feel like I have only had one husband. That's the love story of my Midwestern prince. I miss my Rev.

LAUNCH PAD V: HARD LANDINGS

Deep and Heartbreaking

Hard landings were not lighthearted or fun times in my life. Life may be lived chronologically, but my collective life reflections are all over the place. I wish I could say my reflections are going to feel exciting, crazy, and invigorating. They're not! They weren't lived that way, and I don't want you to be bamboozled. For those who have experienced leaps of sickness, caregiving, loss and death, this section may bring back flashbacks.

I delve into my own searing flashbacks to help you, not to haunt you. Time doesn't heal all wounds, especially those of crushing pain. I will say time helps you get to the light. What light, you ask. The much-needed light at the end of a very long and drawn-out tunnel. Time, whether a little or a lot of it, is up to you. The tunnel requires patience, faith, and tissues for the hot tears. Some leaps you make and others just show up.

The Upside Down of 2010

The year 2010 will forever ring in my ears. Windy squalls, little girls, and little boys don't prepare you for the hurricanes that come to test you. It's like a big, unannounced life exam and you didn't take meticulous notes, you didn't memorize questions and answers, and you most certainly didn't ask the teacher when you should expect the exam. Most of us undoubtedly flunk. I know I flunked.

There is a reason my children hold 2010 in their memory banks as the turning point of all of our lives. On June 15, 2010, William Helm experienced a stroke. He didn't die, but life as we knew it did. The blood constriction on the right side of his brain turned every part of his body and our days on an axle. Mere seconds impacted us for a lifetime. We became upside down. The world kept spinning; we just got left behind.

I appreciate change. I just never like changes that come out of nowhere. Our little family had already been through a lot with Rev's failing health prior to that point. He wasn't a sickly man, but he had his share of ailments. Our family was getting its footing at the end of 2009, as we were among the millions who lost their homes during the housing crisis. Our Flagship Drive home, our life, our friends, and our neighborhood were all gone. We also had to say goodbye to our dog, Seafus. Losing my doggie son cut the hardest. There wasn't a day for almost a year I didn't think of him. Everything in leaving Flagship was heartbreaking.

It felt like we were receiving the fury of fiery darts. In the course of time, we began adjusting to our beautiful new home. God gave us a magnificent new rental property and neighborhood. He made the sting of the farewell a little more tolerable with this huge house of grandeur. Our tight-knit family was surviving when out of nowhere came the stroke. It hit us like a sonic boom! It physically hit him, but it took us all down. It was like we were in a boxing ring and no one had warned us to bob and weave. God was our fortress, but our commander in chief was down in the middle of the ring. We as the corner were flying toward him, pushing, and pulling to get him up, back standing, fighting, responding—anything close to normalcy. He couldn't help himself.

Seeing him flailing in his weakened state, we knew the trips down the highway, the speaking engagements, the get-up-and-go Rev we knew were all of the past. We didn't care about any of that; we just wanted him to be okay. We wanted him to be who he was made to be, a husband, father, brother, preacher, and friend.

The stroke didn't impact Rev's speech or cognition. God left those intact. William and I were so grateful. With any brain injury, the brain has to heal and recover. His emotions were all over the place. The voices of certain loved ones made him cry. The appearance of certain people made him cry. Hearing Diana Ross made him cry. There was no rhyme or reason to it. Noises, music, and sounds hurt his head. He would become irritated that we didn't understand how the unrecognized noises of life were hurting him.

He loved music, reading, and the preached word so much. The loss of them all was a constant piercing to him. The stroke took his independence and so much more that he didn't believe he would ever get back. My man had so many things that forged his manhood. Until those things were gone, he didn't know they were part of his makeup.

Until his brain healed, he couldn't tolerate a lot. He loved his family. He cherished all of us pulling together. He seemed remorseful we were going through all of it. He wasn't used to being taken care of. He wasn't used to feeling such fear. Things that never would have frightened him before the stroke now did. In his recovery, he suffered with paranoia and fear of falling, having another stroke, injuring himself, or having a car accident. Driving in the dark scared him. Me driving all the time frightened him. He was always concerned if I had rested enough before driving. The stroke had nothing to do with an accident in the car, but this fear of an accident plagued him. To this day, I am not sure why.

The new normal was difficult. Everything was new to him and to us. We didn't know how to help. We didn't know how to be there for him. And we didn't know how to be the family we were. What could we laugh about? What were the boundaries? Would we ever clown on each other again? He still was there, but he was not the same. He was injured. I was living off no sleep. Living on Cheerios and Capri Suns. I made it. I didn't need any diet programs. I just lived on exhaustion and lost tons of weight. Life for us all was one foot in front of the other.

I tried my best to help the kids be normal and to keep our household afloat. I had to hold down the fort or the fort would crush us. My workplace during those months was phenomenal. Thank you USCIS OIT and my NetStar-1 Team. I gained new sisters and brothers during this time; my clients and coworkers became family. These guys: Ledora, Lee, Beth, Fayre, Nick, Leslie, and Jess just rallied around me. I had an acquisition work team of incredible people who I will treasure forever. Family is beyond blood.

Rev's family mustered during this crisis. Bill, as they called him, was their anchor of the five of them. Joyce was Mama Bear. She took care of the kids when their Mom and Dad worked. Each of them came and helped in their own way. It was my brother-in-law, David, who was with me as Bill had his stroke diagnosed. It fully manifested in a doctor's office that Dave and I struggled all morning to get him to. He could barely walk. When he lost his strength in the doctor's office, they sent him by ambulance to the hospital next door. Only then was he finally diagnosed twenty-four hours later with the stroke. We had gone for an ER visit at this same hospital a few days prior and to another doctor visit. Even during this ER visit, the CT scan said he had not had a stroke. The medical team could see differently. I was adamant to not let him leave without getting help this time. He was exhibiting left-sided weakness which indicated the brain was injured in his right hemisphere. There had been 3 CT scans over that past couple of weeks that stated he had not had a stroke. Word to the wise – advocate strongly if you know something is wrong with you or your loved one. An MRI is the right equipment to pinpoint a stroke occurrence.

Rev's oldest sister, Joyce, came first. Joyce was a lifelong educator and Faith's second mom. She birthed no children from her body but she nurtured hundreds. Joyce made her way from Peoria, Illinois, and was there for the home care training. She and I would ensure there was no talk of sending Rev to long-term care facility. Over our dead bodies. We Helms would marshal. I was a Helm by marriage, but my blood was Helm through and through now. Joyce, my two small kids, and I would hold Rev down. His early days home were crazy and life threatening at times. The medications were working against him.

The medications prescribed had side effects of constant diarrhea and lowering his blood pressure dangerously low. I was second-guessing whether I had done the right thing. The doctors and specialists had no answers. I worked for weeks researching medication fact sheets and trial notes with a nurse case manager. We had to figure out what was happening and why. Finally, after months, I located information that showed how two of the medications had trial studies which Black men experienced diarrhea. Mystery solved. The doctors altered the medication and the constant plague of diarrhea ended. Praise God!

It was never a joy for Rev to have anyone besides me clean him. Faith was in elementary school, and she was trooper. She would know her dad pooped and get up to grab wet wipes, diapers, and a plastic bag. She was a great helper. Rev didn't like having his siblings do any support below his waistline. The kids and I tried to jump up to take care of that whenever it happened.

As he got stronger, we were relieved of some of those duties. He was struggling with his dignity and wanted to regain it as soon as possible. No man wants that experience, but that was where we were.

During the hardest of these times, another special person entered my life. Nothing tells you how frazzled you are like your hair. I have a head full of it and when I'm exhausted, the last thing I bother with is my do. Enter Theresa, my longtime friend, confidant, and hairstylist. Her salon was a couple blocks from our new house. I couldn't travel long distances to go to my former hairstylist, Gina.

I loved Gina, but traveling an hour to her salon was out. Rev was too fragile. I learned Theresa did all types of hair. I introduced myself to her one afternoon. I came to get a touch-up. She sat me down in her chair and looked at my hair and said it showed stress.

I said, "My husband just had a stroke." We became sisters from that point on. She convinced me to stop perming my hair and go natural. We talked week after week. For over a decade, we've been each other's listening ear. She jokes with people that she's crazy, but Theresa is anything but crazy. She is more grounded and wiser than most people. God uses her for every person who sits in her chair. I'm a living witness. Me being known by people at my county recreation center as the Woman with Hair is thanks to *HairbyTheresa*.

Missing in Action

I'm not going to rehash the details of the 2010 stroke further. There were multiple missed diagnoses, medical training, and support. Rev had shown symptoms weeks earlier than the final diagnosis and hospitalization. The way to that long and tortured diagnosis was a full shit show. Stroke awareness was MIA, but now hospitals and medical care providers are better educated.

Another MIA category were Christian people. We did get support at the beginning, but for a long-term illness, there was more lip-service than real support. Something about sacrificial giving, help and missions escapes the body of Christ. They don't escape Jesus Christ, just His ad-hoc followers. Inconvenience is an Achilles' heel to our soldiers. Our family learned the hard lesson of that. People who didn't dawn the doors of a church house showed kindness when others with pew burns stayed on the sidelines. I guess that's why pews are so comfortable—a lot of butt coddling. We could count on our fingers people that stayed with us during grief, illness, struggle, and pain. Our experience and perspective aren't unique. Am I lying, God? I believe He would put a message in the clouds: *Not at all.*

Fair weather Christians are a dime a dozen. Tragedy and heartbreak expose who are God's genuine followers and who are not. Rev told me years ahead of time who would be there for us and who would not. He wasn't a genie, but he nailed it! He said Pam would be there for us and he was so right.

This section is probably darker than you would have gathered. Don't get me wrong. People helped, but only so much. I am not bitter or upset. I am shining a light on an area in which we as the body of Christ have to do better. As a former wife to a drug addict, I wrongly isolated myself to my own detriment. I didn't isolate with Rev who had a chronic and terminal illness. People saw, people knew, but they stayed away. The ones that showed up were a blessing. We went through caregiving in plain sight. No one with eyes and ears could say they didn't know we were struggling.

I found both experiences isolating. They were different flips of the coin. From first grade on we learned to think of others and pretend to walk a mile in another person's shoes. Caregiving shoes are for tired feet. Not many want to wear them. Uncomfortable shoes are not for the faint of heart. The kids and I know. We wore them for a long time. We understood no one wanted to push wheelchairs, cut up meats, clean linens or lead the blind. If you don't have to, what in your heart would have you jump to offer. Jesus, in your heart would. It's easier to be MIA than sacrifice. No one here in this realm will call you on it. *God sees and know all. He knows what He's called His children to see, do and be.* He was way ahead of us all. He fashioned a little girl named Faith with the heart He would use for his manservant. Our God is always steps ahead of us.

The last MIA to discuss are spouses. This generation has a spouse MIA problem. This was not the case with us, but we saw so many others walk away in a crisis. These days, spouses with sick children and sick partners walk away. That's a shame. Sickness and setbacks are pivotal and life altering. You see the makeup of your spouse when sickness and hardship come. As a wife, I took my vows very seriously. Rev and I were one flesh from the beginning and until the end. There was never a thought that I would ever leave him. That is not the case for many spouses today. The facilities and divorce courts are full of people throwing in the towel. Life is too hard. They didn't sign up for hard. Hello! The vows "in sickness and in health" are there for a reason. Today our uniquely written vows avoid language on suffering. No sickness and in health for the 21st Century.

The vows couples made before God are for wedding cake and frosting. Sickness test love for a lifetime. Spouses today are fitted for running shoes and not concrete boots. The leap of commitment is taken with an exit strategy (a backdoor clause.) Real love stays. Lust runs. My Mom and Dad may have been an unlikely pairing, but they stayed the course. I finished until death parted us.

The Weight of Faith

The weight of caregiving in the later years of Rev's stroke recovery, and illnesses fell on our younger daughter, Faith. She didn't get to have the fun of a childhood. I had so many roles and the weight spilled over onto the only other person in the house at the time. Faith was the only person willing and able to share the exhausting load. She was a child like I had been with my own Dad. Did God allow her birth because he knew, Rev and I would both need her for this season? Was she here for the then and now—for me?

Did God want me to relive my childhood winepress in the eyes of my own daughter? There has to be more to this repeat. Was there a lesson I missed? Why bring Faith into this harsh go-around? I never learned those answers. I just knew my winepress revisited had Faith in the trenches with me. I was grateful for her help and companionship. It was a firefight and I could not have done it without her.

I didn't know the fractures being created in her by our collective lean. Rev and I both would make our constant requests. She was always there, and always willing. She never said, "stop, this is too heavy." How could I not realize I was breaking her? How could I not recognize my early childhood in hers? History was a cruel replicator. I was creating a sequel to my own horror flick. Was Faith afraid to find her Dad dead like I felt? Wasn't my experience enough? Why did she get the same sucker punch? God, wasn't mine enough?

My childhood caregiving was short but nonetheless, terrorizing. Albani and Faith initially shared the load for the stroke recovery. That was brief because Albani was headed to college and an independent life of her own. She was gone. I could not hamper Albani's progress. My younger daughter and I would shoulder life care for our wounded giant. The house, the responsibilities, would be on Faith and me.

From 2010 to 2021, from elementary school to her third year in college, Faith provided constant caregiving for her Dad. She worked non-stop while other kids played and did sports. She heard her Dad's callers say, "let me know if there is anything I can do." Fake support. She worked during the thrill of Obama. She worked during the chaos of Trump. She worked during the crisis of the pandemic. You name it, she worked through it.

She recently opened up about the haunt of having her Uncle David break the news of her Dad's hospitalization. I'm sure he did it in the most compassionate way he could. There is no good way for a fragile elementary school child to hear her Dad is in the hospital and the man she knew him fully to be is not there. The person is the same on the inside, but the outside is never to return again.

I don't know how I could have been in two places so I could have been the one to hold and comfort her as she got the news. There was no way to split myself in half to be with Rev and be with Albani and Faith that day. Everyone needed me. I needed *me*, but I would have to wait. Thank you, David, for being there to help me during that fateful day. I could not have done it all without you.

During this time, Anita the Rock wasn't allowed to have a meltdown. I told myself that, but my body didn't listen. Sure, any normal wife would have allowed herself to, but my lie of fine, repressed emotions, and moving like a freight train were all activated. I was in the middle of a five-alarm fire and I needed to take care of everyone, just not me.

The Trap of Normalcy

On top of being a father and husband, Rev was the associate pastor of Resurrection Baptist Church, Reston, VA. The church was about an hour from our home. After being diagnosed with a stroke and being relocated to a rehabilitation hospital, he wanted us to go to church like normal. He demanded it.

So Sunday after Sunday, we worshiped. For him, it was more important our worship routine remain as normal as possible. What? Nothing was normal for Albani, Faith, or me, but we did as we were told. We worshiped and we heard the preached word. We went to eat at our normal Longhorn Steakhouse, where we ate for the last twenty years. I would take Rev a meal for him and his nursing attendant. Nothing with us was ever by the book.

Maybe the reason so few reached out to us was because I was portraying the lie of fine. I was comforting people and saying we were doing okay while Rev was in the hospital. Faith saw I was being the anchor. She played the assistant anchor.

My charade was found out sooner rather than later. The exhaustion, anxiety, and crumbling materialized one Sunday morning when my arm got numb and I thought I was having a stroke. I called an ambulance. I learned later that my two kids were terrified, as I was taken. They hid on the floor of my walk-in closet, praying and comforting each other. Pam was called again to rescue me. She came, organized my kitchen with dinner, and put me to bed. I had half the congregation and my family sitting on the couch in my bedroom. We watched the Grammys that night. I kept juggling my many roles, often working on vapors.

Considering 2010 and my ambulance ride, my reflection on Faith is that the weight can be too much. I have let both of my daughters know to ask for help. I have shown them running on fumes is not healthy or the right way to live. I'm learning lessons in my fifties that I should have learned in my earlier years, but I wasn't prepared for the life exam when it hit. Like I said, I felt I flunked. I just hope my girls will be okay for the long run.

Disappointing Earthquakes

The year 2010 was hard and the experience could have broken me, but it didn't. It was so much. Rev said he believed I thought he was going to die, but I never thought that. I thought we were going to go through the hardest test of our faith. That ended up being true for us all.

I thought the life exam would have been shorter. I admit I was wrong. That hurricane lasted only to be replaced by a tidal wave. Rev's health began to deteriorate and it was nothing to do with the stroke. Long-term diabetes had impacted his kidney function. We accepted the reality that he would need dialysis. People live long lives with dialysis. We thought Rev would start dialysis by his seventies. He was in his mid-sixties, so we had a little time. His physical body was showing signs of stress. His legs and ankles started swelling. I became a master at massage. His bloodwork was more abnormal than usual. He was crashing on different fronts, but Rev remained Rev.

We were in and out of hospitals for one reason or the other during the thick of the 2020 pandemic. I got permission to be with Rev at all times as his caregiver. I read up on the guidance and had my letters if questioned or told to leave. After we had a really rough night when Rev was barely breathing, he and I agreed we needed to head to the hospital in Maryland. Rev hated hospitals. He cried to me one time that I was going to take him there and he wouldn't leave. We agreed that if he was ever so sick and hospice was ever on the table, I would bring him home.

Upon arrival at the hospital I had to wait in the ER entrance. This was our first time coming in a critical situation. After about an hour, the doctors came out to tell me they thought he was not going to make it. They thought his breathing trouble was because of COVID. I explained his breathing was off because he needed his first round of dialysis to remove the fluid and it was not COVID. I told the doctors to call the kidney specialist on call. I had just alerted the kidney specialist we were in the ER. The ER doctor called the kidney doctor and Rev was prepared to be admitted for the dialysis. They allowed me back in the room with him. His breathing was in the low 70s, but they gave him oxygen. We braced ourselves for being inpatient and having the first dialysis. A mini surgical procedure had to be completed before the dialysis.

There was a slight bleed that didn't stop. The doctors had to take Rev back and do more to stop it. We didn't know it at the time but the inability to clot and the bleeding was an indicator of the tidal wave to come. He was finally able to start the ramp up for the dialysis. Seeing his swollen legs go down to the size they had been when Rev was an athlete seemed miraculous. He looked normal again. He felt better. He could breathe better. Both of us were so relieved to finally have something help him.

We had to find a good dialysis center in Virginia. After a few bumps in the road, we found a clean and well managed dialysis center. The center needed to be close enough to our home because I was still working full-time. I have had incredibly acquisition teams over the years from DHS and NIH/NITAAC. I was juggling and taking Rev to dialysis during lunch and picking him up after work. None of this was easy.

The transition of going to dialysis three days a week for four hours a pop was jarring but manageable. Whatever came our way, we just figured it out. We wanted Rev to be okay. He never quit and we didn't either. As we were easing into our new routine, we received news as we were driving home from a kidney specialist appointment in Maryland. We were told that we had to immediately go to the nearest ER. *Now what?*

The kidney doctor we had seen just thirty minutes before got on the phone to explain that Rev's bloodwork showed his hemoglobin was five. That's a horrible number. They said go to the hospital immediately and do not pass go—Rev could have a heart attack at any time. Rev was sitting in the seat chilled and felt fine. He was grateful to be headed home. We did go home and got something to eat. We then went to the ER at Fort Belvoir. The medical doctors agreed Rev needed to get a blood transfusion to get his numbers up to seven. The first of many future transfusions was completed.

Unbeknownst to us, the entry site for the dialysis couldn't be used for the blood transfusion. Rev had running veins and the many unsuccessful pricks were scaring the skin for needle access. Because of this, another procedure to implant a port was ordered. Getting the port in was its ordeal only to have the smell of an infection rush us into emergency surgery to remove it. This is when I was identified by the surgical team as "Nurse-Wife."

Russian Roulette

Rev had so many holes in his poor body. Each of these surgical procedures was life threatening because his platelets were also low and his blood was not clotting. That was the beginning of a mysterious blood illness. It wasn't enough that he was recovering from a stroke, living with diabetes, in chronic kidney failure, and masking up from a deadly pandemic. Now we were battling an unknown blood disease that ravaged his blood like cancer but wasn't. Dear Lord, really? What kind of Job-like leap was this?

It was like Satan was playing Russian roulette with all the chambers loaded. The weekly blood results showed something was killing Rev. The doctors didn't know what. We were sent to an oncologist and a hematologist for test after test. Nothing revealed cancer, but the bloodwork showed the vulture was mimicking cancer. Everything felt like a downhill spiral. We kept our life as normal as we could during a killer pandemic. Rev ministered online as the Pastor of Resurrection Baptist Church during the years after his stroke. Our family loves to eat and eat very well. We figured if were in the midst of the last suppers, we were going to eat good ones.

During that time, we watched Home and Garden TV. The shows were calming and we could just relax. We got into them so much, Rev allowed me to renovate much of the house and the backyard. We just paid paycheck to paycheck. Jorge, our contractor was in our pandemic bubble. His wife was pregnant and we both played it safe. I think Rev knew renovating the house was a stress reliever for me. In hindsight, it certainly was. I also think Rev wanted the house to be updated the way I wanted it. He wanted everything fixed before something happened with him. Faith had just left for her freshman year in college when the pandemic sent her back home from college. She was going to class on zoom and that was hard enough. In addition in her off-time, she was providing caregiving again. Faith never got the much needed break even during her college experience. Albani and my future son-in-law Broderick were together. Everyone was safe and accounted for.

During an oncologist visit, we were offered a palliative care doctor. Palliative care doctors treat chronic and terminal patients. I knew this. I'm not clear if Rev understood all of the language being thrown at him. I said we would accept that care and the social support it would bring. The doctor we got was incredible. He helped us navigate all of these specialists and translate Rev's intentions and wishes for his life goals. He wanted to preach for as long as he could. It's hard to see those 2021 videos of Rev's teaching because he was so ill. His color, his breathing, and his stamina were so frail. Preaching was the one thing he wanted to muster all his strength to do. The doctor was so supportive and I was so grateful for him.

The palliative care doctor was refreshing. He and his team listened and were responsive. All the doctors during this journey were not always the best. Some were dismissive. I was taking care of William full-time and they were treating him at best for 15 minutes. I was researching and reviewing medical data to try to find out what was happening to Rev. I would review side effects and medical information on offered treatments before providing decisions. We declined cancer treatments that could possibly kill Rev faster than the course of the illnesses. I am not a fan of chemo or certain drugs when the doctor is unsure. They are "practicing" medicine. More than once we declined treatment options and we'd hear the doctor concur or a nurse give us the nod that we did the right thing. Why the hell did they offer them?

One afternoon after tests, specialists, multiple visits, and no diagnosis, we asked the senior oncologist to let us know Rev's life expectancy if this blood disease went on. I knew when his resident had offered a palliative care doctor that this was our last saga. They didn't say it, but I wanted to hear what they were not saying. I was not trying to be cold in asking the question on the time, I just wanted to hear what they were saying behind the scenes.

He responded that we were looking at eighteen months if nothing changed. I don't think Rev was paying attention to what was said. He was looking at his TV show. I repeated what the doctor said and Rev didn't react. He believed his life was in God's hands and not the doctors. We decided we weren't going to live in fear. We would take each day as it came.

We hoped the doctors would figure out what was destroying his blood and we'd be back on track for just having dialysis. Trying to support them finding the disease meant three painful bone marrow tests, countless blood tests, infusions, and new drugs.

Rev didn't have cancer, but we were living in the cancer infusion center. I worked remotely in his infusion cubicle while he got blood. I took meetings in the private bathroom. We were together as much as possible. If he had to be hospitalized, so was I. I had my work gadgets, his supplies, and favorite treats to make a hospitable stay bearable.

You may say to yourself, who hopes for just needing dialysis? We did. We knew people who were on dialysis for years, but the mystery of this blood disease was not giving us much hope. Rev's quality of life was dismal. I was in the boat with him. Having him by my side made my boat float. I was at peace with that. I studied bloodwork on all the alphabet soup of those numbers every week. I was performing comparisons on +/- of blood tests from the hospital, the infusion center, and the dialysis center.

None of the reports showed the blood getting better. His platelets were so low we had to be careful of any cut because he could bleed out. He officiated two funerals during COVID. He got a cut on his ankle before we left for one of them. I bandaged it up, but I was terrified. I watched his ankle for signs of blood the entire service. I was praying not to contract COVID and not to have Rev bleed. Funerals during COVID were unbelievable. We felt like we were playing with a death sentence every time we left the house. Rev believed in supporting his members at any cost.

With blood transfusions, the body only allows the invasion of foreign blood for so long, until it doesn't. In the early weeks, this process was helpful, then his body got wise and rejected the blood. Things went from bad to worse.

Nurse-Wife

The news of the blood rejection meant we were entering the final phases of this disease. By then, I had a little more support in our home than Faith. We received support from the Veteran Affairs aides. Rev was granted eleven hours per week. That's not a lot, but it something. I had gotten their help years earlier and our two aides, Judith and Juliet, were my life savers. Judith was a veteran and had seen patients change from viable to hospice. This was new for Juliet. In addition to the aides, we also had fantastic nursing care in the hospital and at home. Our medical team and care support became family. When the time for Rev's transition came all of them were crushed. We were so fortunate that most of our nursing care and support team were Christians. They knew they would see Rev again.

Rev spoiled and loved every one of them. Our house was a revolving door for nurses, caregivers, Jorge, and restaurant deliveries. I don't know if all my medical training qualifies me for anything, but I am the ghetto doctor of my family. I had surgeons teach me and their residents about wound care. I stayed in hospitals for days at a time monitoring, changing, and observing. I would learn what I needed from the hospital RNs so I knew what to do in a crisis back at our home.

When I stayed at the hospitals, I participated in the hallway doctors' round-discussions. I waited until they finished and then followed up with my questions and clarification to the specialists. I was Rev's private onsite nurse observing everything. I could spot a baby doctor a mile away. When they struggled with something, I would tell them a trick I had seen from the many specialists and doctors before.

When Rev underwent surgeries during COVID, I hid out in the corridors, waiting for the surgeons to finish and tell me everything was okay. They knew I was there waiting and they came out to give me the news. My heart would skip beats waiting to know if he made it through yet another procedure. That became my life.

One transport person during a hospital visit, seeing me prep Rev to go downstairs for a four-hour dialysis session, called me obsessed. I was not obsessed. I was a loving wife, best friend, and manager. I managed for a profession. My husband was going to get my best management attention until he left this realm. Those days, weeks, and months were daunting. During the pandemic, we all were fearing a virus. We were coming and going in and out of medical facilities. I didn't know the full strain on Faith. She was caring our load and trying to go to virtual classes.

I was trying to work full time and maintain as much normalcy as was reasonable. I keep using the word normalcy because that's what I wanted. We were having virtual church services. I was keeping up with my podcast, Milkshake Mondays. We were moving and living as best anyone could during a global pandemic and worldwide lockdown. We were in a whirlwind of existence. May be to the outside world that appeared obsessed. I called it survival.

The Mask of Fine

The slap of reality was when Faith admitted to me that she was feeling the same pain, suffering, and reckoning I had experienced with my own Dad dying. I was sharing how I felt about Rev and how it reminded me of my own Dad when I was a kid. Faith said, "So Mom, what do you think I'm going through?"

I was oblivious. It was good I was lying down because if not I would have fallen. I knew she was hurting, and this time was tough. I thought I had shielded her somehow better than my own Mom had shielded me. I hadn't done anything of the sort. I thought being open and talking to her more would help her through this better. She held her mask perfectly in place and I didn't see the truth. She had been living the "I am fine" deception. I did not want that for Albani or Faith. I wanted them both to be okay, but I failed to look beyond the looking glass. I didn't try to draw out of her what she needed from me. I didn't help her open up about what was really hiding behind her layers.

Every now and then, I would let my own emotions out, albeit in the car by myself or in the shower. I didn't let them see toward the end my hurt. I thought I could read people. I missed reading the two most important women in my life. What a revelation in the raw days of hospice. I'm sure both Faith and Albani held their masks tightly. I should have pulled them off.

This blow was cruel. Throughout all of Rev's sicknesses, especially this one, we both had tried to love, communicate, and protect our girls from the suffering. We didn't hide how sick he was. That was evident. We just wanted to keep as much of our family and our normalcy as we could. We had long since given up our pre-stroke life. We even gave up mobility and a whimsical life. Pushing wheelchairs, helping Rev dress, and caring was not easy, but we had our moments of laughter and fun throughout everything. Boy could Rev laugh!

Rev was a talker. He could be frank, silly, and give a lesson all while yelling at the TV. Our girls loved and listened to their Dad all their lives. My love language is communication, and I listened to him all the time. He spent a lot of time talking to Albani. She was newly engaged and living on her own. As he got sicker, he couldn't speak without having a strange hiccup-belch attack. We never learned what that was about.

He always talked to both girls all of their lives. He told us story after story. When we begged, he would yell, "that's Wayne May!" He had his share of stories from Rev. and Mrs. Hughes, Zita, his Mom, Dad, Ms. Jewell every sibling, Blenn, Carl, Matt, beautiful Gretchen Johnson, the Melniks and on and on. It was always laughable to hear the fun of Decatur life. If you hadn't heard about snowstorms and Krekel's custard you hadn't been around Rev. Memories are fun.

As he got sicker, Rev was eager and excited when Albani called the house. His voice got animated and you would hear, CUPCAKE! I could tell he wanted to talk to her. I think he realized his talks about life, marriage, and what to expect were drawing to a close. We never talked directly as a family about death, but he knew, and we did too.

We were not a typical preacher's family. We allowed ourselves to live honestly and without legalism. Rev and I were parents, not friends. We guided our daughters and they lived their own lives with their own consequences.

Rev was so sick in the end. He wanted Faith (aka Pudding), and Albani, (aka Cupcake), to be okay. He didn't see how Faith was hurting under the pressure. In hindsight, I think that's good because that would have killed him on the inside. He once said to me, "I'm sorry I'm sick."

I stopped him and told him taking care of him was the privilege of my life. Even knowing what I know now, I would marry William Helm all over again.

William and I tried to shield Albani and Faith from the worry about his death. They knew he was really sick. We should have all sat down and talked about how we all felt about the eventuality of it. We dealt with the looming death separately or some of us not at all. The truth is, no matter what protection we could have tried or at what age, death crushes. I had failed the Express Your Feelings class as a teenager, and I flunked it for a second time in my fifties. This time I brought my girls along.

For men and women struggling with mental health, seeing a therapist, and getting counseling is a must. It's healthy. Diving into how we feel is important. Find your safe space. Not all counselors in our lives have degrees and hang shingles on the door. I applaud and encourage support from licensed professionals in mental health. That said, some people refuse that lane. We should really consider doctors specializing in mental health for those issues. We wouldn't go to a vet for brain surgery. We wouldn't go to the grocery clerk for car repairs. And it doesn't make sense to go to non-mental health professionals for emotional help. Whatever lane you choose, get help.

Too Little, Too Late

We did not learn William's diagnosis of myelodysplastic syndrome (preleukemia) until he was close to death. The diagnosis came too late for him. He was too far down the road to departure. I used my phone back in 2021 to tape the doctor telling us the news. I recently found the audio on my phone and heard the recording. It's been years since hearing those words. Hearing the doctor explain the treatment alternatives was sad at that point. We waited for a diagnosis only to get it almost two years too late.

Maybe a healthy person going down that road could take advantage of that alternative, but not William. He was too beat, too frail. Any new measure was ludicrous. He already had no quality of life and the treatment would have had him in a hospital for two weeks at a time with the mere hope something would change. I wanted no more practicing on my prince.

William Helm struggled and fought mightily until he experienced another stroke July 2021. We didn't know this time because the effects were masked by all the other trauma he was going through. This one was a bleeding stroke. By the time we knew it, he was affected with no options. We took him home for comfort care (hospice). I put the word out in a video. I didn't have any strength to make dozens of calls and give explanations.

From July 17, 2021, to August 2, 2021, Rev stayed at home as our family came together. Albani and Broderick, Faith, Darlene (his youngest sister), David and his family, Pam and Kyle, Tina, church family and friends all came. People called to say last farewells by phone. Rev was mostly on pain meds and sleeping. He would open his eyes every now and then. Mainly he would awake around 3:00 a.m. during my shift in hospice, and sometimes he spoke. I mostly read the Bible and sang to him during that time. One time I said while he was sleeping, "You always loved your family." He responded, "Always."

He had his last gasp of speaking when he awoke on a Thursday afternoon and wanted water. He asked Jorge, our construction friend, if he needed anything. That was so Rev. Jorge said, "No, Mr. William." He lay dying and asking someone living do they need anything. No one told me immediately he was awake. I happened to see Judith, our aide, as she was getting the water. I ran downstairs to see him awake and talking.

When I saw him, I said "Hey, *babe*" in a such a high-pitched voice. The excitement and joy rang through me. I didn't think I'd talk to my friend again. He'd been silent for days. He spoke his last time to me that Thursday before his death that following Monday. It was like God allowed his final goodbye. When I gave him his morphine, I felt like I was sending him to his final goodbye.

During those last couple of days, he had awful seizures. When the first seizure happened, the reaction naturally was for everyone to say call 9-1-1. I calmly explained there is no calling 9-1-1 at this stage. The doctor and nurse had explained what medicine to provide at this stage. We were waiting for the end. I slept alongside him the last night and tried to feel the tremors from the seizures starting. I tried to medicate him as soon as possible to help him suffer less. That was all the could be done for my Prince. He was suffering and I did not want him to stay for this. I miss him all the time, but I could never want him back here to suffer. He is painless with Christ.

As he was taking his last breath and his blood pressure was ebbing away, we just kept saying we loved him. Jesus loved him. On August 2, 2021, at 12:51 p.m., Rev. William Dallas Helm took his voyage to be with the Lord. I got on Facebook Live and told everyone. The mortician retrieved his body and we released balloons.

LAUNCH PAD VI:
LOSS AND DEATH

I'm still learning many things after the death and loss of people I love, especially Rev. I wish I could be definitive and say the lessons are final, but they are not. As soon as I think I've booked a lesson and can move on, a grief drive-by occurs, and I realize I'm still learning. Here are five lessons:

Lesson 1: Memories Fade

It's hard to believe that little things you experience day in and day out are traveling further in the distance. You think they NEVER will, not on your watch, but time erodes them. When I see a picture or video or hear a story, it will bring a remembrance back, but some things are losing prominence. The person you never forget, but all the little, tiny, ever-present details are slipping away.

Case in point, I saw a picture of my husband's hand and the fingernails, the ridges, the small scars—the little things about which I know the when, why, and how. I don't think about these things anymore and they disappear as irrelevant in my brain. He's not irrelevant, but those thousand little memories of his hand have become irrelevant. Life in the now overshadows the life of then. That lesson hurts because in all the love we hold dear, the present and living have a way of doing that.

One of my most treasured loved ones, William Helm, said, "You'll forget me."

I said, "NEVER!" Maybe through all of his grief, he understood more than I did about forgetting the little things.

Lesson 2: Grief and Heartache

To know love is tremendous. We personify it, but love is bigger than the person. When they are gone, we don't know how to grab the parts of it that aren't bound by that missing body, voice, and touch. We throw aside the corny jokes remembered, the lessons and wisdom given, the children born from their lovemaking, and all of those left-behind treasures that take a back seat to them missing.

One day I will be gone, and I want my loved ones to process the pain, then live on. I hope something in my lessons will allow their tears and pain to flow but also push them to get up and keep moving. The people in my life who knew they were dying and leaving me didn't fixate on the aftermath. They loved me in real time. They kept dancing at the party until the music stopped. I'm sure they wanted to talk about their fears and regrets, but they didn't want to start the agony before it had to begin. I love the idea of parents who are dying and have young children leaving behind notes or videos marking different milestones. I treasure all the Bible teachings and sermon videos of Rev. Helm. I can hear his voice, hear the wisdom of his teaching, hear him talk of me, or hear him tell a quirky story for the 100th time. Grief and heartache cannot be ignored;

they both have to be lived. You must understand that part of living is processing dying.

Lesson 3: Overcoming Fear

Fear is a trap of lost hope. I've stumbled down the road of fear because I didn't know what was around the corner for me. Having my missing loved one didn't change the unknowns, but there was a change in the walking. Before the loss, I had a companion in chief. I had someone physically walking the journey with me. Before you think it—I know God is always there and key in my life. In losing someone in death, my life support changed.

My corner of experience that made me feel connected, supported, understood, and valiant was summoned away never to return. The loss made me feel small and more vulnerable. Before the loss, having God and my husband made me feel impenetrable and invincible. What a shield of protection. I had such strength and faith.

With my loved one gone, I had only God. Was I fearful God alone wasn't enough? Did I fear Him seeing how frail I felt? I knew in my loss of my husband he was the stronger and me the weaker. That's the beauty of having two in battle with separate armor. The two becoming one flesh can take the battle side by side and offset each other's weaknesses.

Overcoming fear means asking, "Who would offset my weaknesses now?" In the lesson of the after, I had to trust God wholeheartedly in ways I hadn't done since my youth. Big Anita had forgotten what God did in little Anita with the loss of my Dad. He overcame my emotional blind spots. With the death of my Dad, I felt orphaned even though I had a Mom. God showed me *He was my parent*. With the loss of my husband, I felt alone, even though I had my children. God showed me *I AM your home.*

Fear and pain personify vulnerabilities that were covered up under walls that the loved one's presence painted over. Sure, after the losses in my life I kept one foot in front of the other on the outside, but what was going on within was vastly different. God was seeing masking tape on the outside as He was working on filling the fractures inside my heart. He was shoring me up until I could feel complete again with just Him.

Lesson 4: Keep Hope

Hopelessness is not a solution. In death know that the destination of hopelessness is depression and crumbling. Keep hope. Fight for it even when you feel hollowed out. Remember your loved one would never want you *lost* as the consequence of them dying. They died having hope you would survive this blow.

Find hope and chain it to your being. If you question how to find hope, start with thanking God about everything about the one who you lost. Our loved ones are not lost to Him. Thank God for every little thing they meant to you. In your thankfulness, you will drip vapors of hope in the hollows of your pain. You will in due time find an outpouring of gratefulness to God for the gift He gave to you. That gratefulness will pick your chin upward to Him who stills you, who gives to you, who loves you. In Him will you find true *hope.*

Lesson 5: Questioning

There's a lot of questioning that you can't put into words. The agony of loss is not for words but in tears and unmet longings. You can't put death's questioning to paper, and in reality, you don't know how to put them forward. What now? How? Can I? Do I want to? Why now? God, will you? When? What if? If the questioning is hard, how about the answers, the silence, the waiting? Questioning and the process of it all can be crushing. Therein lies one of the mysteries of death and loss. I will stop now because there is someone further down this road that must have answers. I, dear one, am not there yet.

Winepress Revisited

Was anything revealed in all that? In our weakness, God was made strong. There was no choice about living or being weak in the knees. It was a slow walk to eventuality. Rev and I didn't talk about death. I let him know I wasn't going to bury him because I don't visit graveyards. I can count on one hand the times I have seen my own Dad's burial site.

I don't believe the souls are there, so I'll see them in heaven or I won't. I knew I would see William Helm again. I was trying to pre-grieve if that is even a thing. I would hate to see what my grief would have been if I didn't pre-grieve because what I went through in the aftermath of my best friend's transition was *brutal*.

I didn't have anything left in me but faith. I held hope that I would see my brother again, but I needed grace. I was carrying little Nita so close. I was holding on to her with my bare fingertips. Losing Rev was gutting me worse than losing my Dad had. With Rev, I had the time to tell him all I wanted to tell him.

I remember in the final seconds of his life; the hospice nurse at our house was saying he was still alive. He said keep talking to him. I just kept repeating, "I love you. I love you. I love you."

He looked gone. He looked so far gone. I didn't think I was talking to Rev anymore, but his dead corpse. Nevertheless, I kept repeating my love. Rev had done all he could to hold on to dear life until God took him home. The repeat of this winepress revisited was all too much.

What Holding Back Looks Like

The inside emotions I wrestle with are those of being overwhelmed, disappointed, questioning, doubting, frustrated, and impatient. I'm holding back my heart. I have cried a lot in the past few years, more times than I can count. I am holding my heart back to hopefully protect it from further harm. I know in order to love again I have to let my heart out, but I haven't done such a good job of late or in my past. I'm holding big chunks of it back until I experience the one who will be true and loving back toward it. I'm holding back my passion. Anita wants it, but that part of myself has to be held in stasis. I am holding back the part of me that is aging. My mind is not as sharp and focused as it was in my youth. Duh! I'm holding back the admission and revelation that I am changing. I'm eating healthier, exercising, and taking care of myself, but I'm aging. Theresa is a great colorist!

I'm not my almost 100-year-old mother with her short-term memory lapses, but I see the changes in my mind. My mental agility plays word salad sometimes. The year-to-year changes can be monstrous. Don't get me wrong. I'm still sharp, but I was sharper! It's good I'm getting this book out now because it could have been reduced to a Dr. Seuss nursery rhyme. I am not ready to face the full knowledge of Anita's aging and I hold that back from myself.

I'm holding back my tongue and judgment. If you don't agree, I am. I'm kind of pissed about it too. When you get older, you are expected to be able to let loose. I like to be completely frank and honest, but these pussycats are so soft they cannot handle it. I didn't want to say pussycats, but you know, *political correctness.*

I find myself holding back my pace. I like action and I like speed. Rev said, "You like everything fast and I mean everything!" In fairness, I don't like everything fast, but I do love efficiency and results. I see what those around me don't always. This is apparently true with God Himself. He's been showing me in the last couple of years things in the present that don't happen until the next year. Small things, but things all the same.

Rev told me months before he died, "God is going to slow you down."

I asked him if he was threatening me or warning me.

He said, "It's not a threat. He repeated that God was going to slow me down. Boy was he right. God is telling me my timing is not His. In all honesty, I'm holding back being a little pissed about God's timing.

I'm holding back frustration that I thought I would be married again by now. Rev gave me a year. I said two years. Both of us were wrong. Time has ticked off another year. I'm curious: am I close? God knows I want to be in union again. He knows it and I know He knows who. He is deathly silent. He's not even giving me a hint. I have to wait. Yes, I'm waiting, God. I'm not thrilled, but waiting, nonetheless.

Now you know why waiting is a constant challenge for me. I'm part Energizer bunny, Joyce Meyers, MacGyver, Toni Morrison, and clock watcher. The drive and creativity push me to move. Maybe He wants me to get a lot done without the distraction of a mister. I get that.

I am more in purpose now. This book is an example of that. A Leap of Faith will help more people than a new love. God is right. He is making

His adjustments in me during this process. Case in point, during my wait for my new squeeze, I have had to overcome the battle of envy and jealousy. Can you believe that? For years, people by the droves came to Rev and me and they would say things about being jealous of us. I didn't understand it fully before, but I understand how someone can want what we had. It was truly rare. Be patient Nita. Wait.

Courage to Survive

As I look at the woman in the mirror in this phase, I rarely use the word *courage* related to myself. As you can see, I have been through a lot. Some of you will say I glazed over and rattled off trauma and tragedy with a bunch of commas in between. Why didn't I go into detail? There's pain between every comma. In my speaking sessions, I speak about the five pillars of relationships. As I read the room, as the Holy Spirit leads, I open up about specific stories in detail as needed. When I share, I pour out what's needed for the listeners. I think you've seen I've tried to be honest in sharing my struggles. I don't identify as a victim, but as a survivor. I had the courage to survive.

I don't feel courageous, but when you speak to me in terms of survival I start to think differently. I feel I have mustered the courage to survive. I marshaled courage to pull Albani and myself out of danger. I took hold of courage to make it through dark days. I think me making it through has been due to God and my resilience to persevere. Relying on myself rather than Him is usually how I got into a fix in the first place.

I am grateful for who I have become. I see things through a different lens than most. I am hopeful for the future. I am resourceful and I am joyful. Having the Lord during my struggles made me more courageous even though I was scared for many of the leaps in my life. They didn't all turn out well, as you can see, but in each one I found myself that much closer to who I am.

Those who have everything handed to them and never struggle, seem lost. I see people who appear entitled wandering through life as though no one told them why they exist. They are almost clones of those who have gifted them with too much yet required nothing. Having no responsibilities has left them walking aimlessly with no purpose. They have blinders on for a rudderless existence.

Say what you want to say about trouble and my questionable choices, but I can give an account of my life. The life filled with my questionable choices has been mine. I made it as good and as awful as it's been. Through God's grace I'm still standing. I'm a *survivor.*

What's Percolating Within

Dealing with my feelings can be like dealing with my desk. I know pretty well where everything is supposed to be, but items have been moved out of place. My feelings are within, but sometimes they come out sideways. That happens in grief. Emotions get cluttered when you don't deal with them. When I struggle to feel and express my emotions something on the inside is off balance. Some part of me I've moved around and it's not put back in its rightful place. Anita is overwhelmed with the clutter. Like my desk, only when I get fed up with the chaos do I stop and regroup. *A Leap of Faith* is helping me regroup. Regrouping on the inside often requires some screams and tears. I don't make myself a pillar for others, but when people are falling apart and you are supporting them, a part of you stays in a holding pattern.

Like an ambulance driver racing to the hospital after a pickup, you can be grossed out by what you see, but those emotions have to wait until after you triage and get the patient on life support Well, with me it's time for Anita, the ultimate patient, to take a break. I have gotten other patients through triage. Now it's my turn to put aside the adrenaline and check out what's percolating inside. I need to address my own vitals. All of my own mayhem needs rescuing by God, our Savior. I'm no one's savior. He is.

When you find yourself being His hands and ears, if you're not careful, you can lose yourself. I'm not close to losing myself, but I struggle with the self-expression of No. I can't always say yes to everything I am asked. The people pleaser has to put her foot down.

I minister to others, but I too have to be ministered to. With Rev gone I have to be careful not overcommitting myself. People can constantly ask, take, and pull on you. Ministry and coaching support can drain you if you don't stay connected to the vine. You have to take care of your own emotions too.

I have to allow space for my own "tears" to venture out. In order to empathize with others, I need my own emotions in check. I have to listen for God's direction and His comfort to me. When I'm balanced within then I can help others. The reality is there will be times my emotions have to be tabled until others are okay, but not at the expense of myself. I know the importance and power of prayer—the great *debrief*.

When I'm working and moving like a freight train, I can forget to fill up my own tank. Rev used to say he was giving out but needed to be poured into. I totally get it. I find I have too much going out and not enough healthy coming in. That's the importance of the spiritual *debrief*. He has to fill me. Me teaching Milkshake Mondays helps me *debrief*. God gives me life lessons from His word every week.

Whenever I'm traveling by car, plane, or train, I have a pattern of listening to Christian teachings, reading books, pouring in for my own spiritual filling. Teaching is for my health and strength. This world and its people will take, take, and take from you. At no time do a lot of takers ask you whether there is anything you need.

For the most part, I try to stay even keeled. The cares of this world tend to trap me. I run on high octane, but the world runs on evil diesel. Evil knows time is winding down. There is a fire sale on every corner. People are donning hats, bumper stickers, and commitments to the father of lies. These misplaced labels are being worn by those professing one thing and living another. I walk a fine line myself. I love God, but I'm not conservative. I love people, but I don't like changing pronouns. I teach Jesus, but I'm no doctor. The lanes I travel for ministry are fast, wide, and cunning.

The people God steers me to are oblivious to godly direction and walking blindly through a *wide* gate. This is spiritual warfare. Being outside God's earshot could get me killed. I can't afford having arrows aimed at me and being spiritually out of whack. A lot is percolating within. I appear calm in this battle, but there is nothing calm about spiritual warfare.

Thinking about ministry, teaching, being, going, and serving can pull me off track if I go in my own strength. Oftentimes, when I fool myself to think I'm doing just fine, it's my own spawn that push me back to reality. They get Anita Helm up close and personal. They will be the first to cry foul when I've injured them. I can injure them by having my tank empty or having my perspective and not walking in God's. They will say I hurt them. When they elaborate, they will express how I have been thoughtless or uncaring and turn the tables on me. The truth hurts. God's pruning hurts, but cuts help clarify what's foggy. My attention, respect, compassion, and active listening cannot be less to my own than I would give to a stadium full of strangers.

That my peering friends is the flawed character of Anita L. Helm as told from the story of my myriad *Steel Magnolias* characters. The Anita I want to be and the one who shows up are not the twins found in the mirror. I don't want to hurt people, least of all my baby girls who are now women. I love my small tribe. With William gone, we feel so tiny. He was such a large part.

We felt like twenty people and now we are four. The last thing I want to do is diminish us further. There aren't any reserve recruits in the bunker. I get the message of the dilemma of my unraveling. I have to navigate Anita and not be a people pleaser. I should have known that was part of my diagnosis decades ago. I always thought I was doing what I wanted.

I realized I was doing what I wanted, as others, I believed, expected. That's another balancing act I need to work on. I need to focus on what pleases God. I don't always please Him and I for sure don't always please me. So there it is. Who am I pleasing if not the two of us? Is someone constantly pleasing God? Put your hand down—you aren't either. I get plenty of confrontation and conviction in this realm as it is. My point is I get attitude adjustments from the cheap seats.

On camera, you can believe I have it all together. I don't. Believe me. God works through all of us, and perfection is not His criterion. He's *perfect*. The rest of us are a work in progress. I love how God operates, letting flawed characters proclaim His Son. We get to teach His Scripture as His Spirit guides us. When I teach, it's not me—it's all the Spirit. Off camera, if I could only keep my ear totally attuned and not go off script and ad lib. I desire to live what I teach. Thanks for forgiving and walking with me, Lord.

Fragments

As a young child, I lived in silent heartache with my mother. In my adulthood and now a widow, I visited that same house and there was no silence this time. Our expression was now open. The lie of fine was broken. It took decades and her wanting me to survive my own husband's death for my Mom to open up. She saw I was moving, but I was dazed. It was her knowing what I was feeling and where I was numb that finally let her break open her emotional vault.

She was throwing me a lifeline to pull me close. Like the baby I once was on her breast, she was pulling me close to hear her heartbeat and feel her touch. I was graced with the fruit of it. I needed it now more than ever.

I knew to keep moving. That's what my Mom demonstrated. I knew to keep one foot in front of the other. It didn't matter that my guts were unraveling and my heart broken. The one thing I did know was I wanted support. I wanted grief counseling.

We were in the throes of the pandemic; I was determined to go to grief counseling. Mom's words were supportive, but I needed more. My dear friend and sister Ledora told me about a virtual program her church was involved with called Griefshare. Pandemic-era deaths were jarring. Planning and living through all of it was a lot. I knew I wasn't going to get support onsite, but virtual was better than nothing.

What I did as a child wouldn't be good for me or my daughters. We each went through our separate Griefshare counseling sessions.

During the sessions, I couldn't completely turn off Anita the encourager, the empathetic one. I was hurting, but when I found myself needing to encourage in our sessions, I did. I remember going through the sessions twice.

During the second time I was healthier and could minister. At the end of my last session they asked me to sing. I did. I knew that although supporting a grief ministry would be beneficial for them, that was not what God called me to do in that venue. I started sharing encouragement to those grieving in my blogs and audio tapings. That's how I played my part.

During my grief counseling I remembered the fundamental takeaway: Drink, Eat, Exercise and Rest (DEER). I had my acronym soup to say to myself. "Anita, have you done your DEER today?" I'd reply, "Yep, keep it moving, baby." Loneliness and losing your identity is hard. Not being a wife messed with my identity. I found talking with other widows comforting. While in the newness of grief, my brain was functioning but in fragments of Anita. The whole Anita was not in synch.

Until you go through trauma and tragedy, what I am saying won't make sense. Time doesn't heal all wounds. But time and reordering the pieces, the fragments, and the pain does. I was in my regrouping. It took processing and digesting that I was here and Rev was not. My mind, emotions and body fragments took a time to reorder his absence. Some of my fragments and his are still swirling inside, but I'm working the process. There are moments even now when a fragment will float by and I grab it and say, "Where did you come from?"

The Love Is Different

Favor from God has been occurring during this season of restoration. I was meeting people only God could have introduced me to. Lots of people! If not for Rev's death, I would not have met some of the people I now call friends.

Case in point, I was showering at the pool and I overheard a conversation about marriage, love, and starting over. I had to ask her about her comment about love. She revealed she had been twice a widow. She was a senior. I asked her how it was to love another. She helped me in her words so tenderly to say the love is different. She said she lost two husbands and the second one was the love of her life. In my mind, I went, "Huh?" That conversation and awakening was helpful, not because I am looking to meet the love of my life, but because the possibility exists. I'm still living. I don't know what is in store for me.

At this writing, William has been the love of my life. Until hearing that woman's words, I never imagined I could have even more love in my future. I am open to love again. I don't know if that will be a gift God gives me or not. That's another mystery yet to unfold. Should an unknown love or lover be grander than what I already have experienced, I say bring it on. That's a tall mountain to climb, but what an adventure that would be! I am a silly romantic and my hopefulness is to have possibilities. My hope doesn't diminish my past love. The love will be different.

LAUNCH PAD VII:
A FULL CIRCLE

I Want to Be Loved Again

William and I bonded on so many levels. It was so fast and so seamless. We had a friendship that lasted his lifetime. I have loved and been loved. Thank you, God! I know what real love takes, and I am whole enough for the next journey.

In my thoughts on this being a full circle for little Nita, I know a few things I want to be clear about. I don't want to settle this time. I don't want to get it wrong. If this is my last time, I want to make it count. Let me be honest on my state of mind. I am questioning. I know I am supposed to be assured, seasoned, and knowledgeable. The reality is, sometimes those teenage doubts creep into my very middle-aged thoughts. By now you expect more from me. I do too, but I'm opening up to the truth. I can't put on the lie of fine for this truth. You expect great wisdom. So do I. I don't always have it in this area of my own heart. I seek more grace from God than you may be willing to afford me.

I am not sure who rings the bell that says times up for grief. I feel whole. I want to love again. Does that ring the bell?

You don't have an answer. That's okay because I am prayerful. I'm mustering all my hope and strength to wait. I want to be found by who God has for me. He's told me no already as my eyes wander. This time I must listen. Here's what I know today about what I look for in the man I will vow to love again until death do us part:

I need to be able to trust the intimacy of that man's love and reverent fear of the Triune God (Father, the Son Jesus Christ, and the Holy Spirit).

I need a thoughtful and giving man with a purpose from God that I can walk alongside for the journey.

I need mutual family connection. We are one and we have our children. Not his children and my children, but our children, our family. We need to commit to love and nurture our family side by side. That can never change when one of us goes home to God before the other. I need evolving spiritual, physical, emotional, and communication. I need commitment and honesty.

Borrowed Time

For Anita 2.0, it's time to focus on more than temporary things. My romantic bug has to wait. I am not thrilled but that's the reality. For these unwritten chapters, I have many high expectations. I want to live the chapters before my unknown finish line. Ultimately, I want to hear God say, "Well done. You finished all your pages." The thing about finishing is you are not sure what you are supposed to start. God knows my finish line. He knows the ending from the beginning in everything about my life, but I'm guessing leap by leap.

He's put so much into me. He's given me incredible gifts. I'm trying to leave none of them wasted. I'm asking God whether I am using all of my gifts fast enough to get done what He wants. Am I close to using everything up? Have I done what I was sent here to do? I want to fulfill my purpose. God sees centuries like we see moments. I have so few moments left in this realm. I'm on borrowed time with a stopwatch ticking in my head.

People say all the time things like they are bored and have nothing to do. Are you kidding me? I hear people say the scriptures are boring, the scriptures are confusing, and the Bible is outdated. People say there's nothing after death. We just die and are worm food. Jesus is a White man's religion. Nobody loves me.

Do you hear all of this mess? Do you hear all the lies the devil has cruising around this planet? My head hears, "Tick tock, Nita, do something. People don't understand God's word. Tick tock, Nita, teach something. People are confused. Tick tock, Nita, give something."

There's so much to do all across this great big marble. People of faith are sitting on the sideline, letting their pew-stained carcasses grow while the few carry the load. The 80/20 rule is smothering the church. Too many are watching the fight. The tick tock of my borrowed time is getting louder and moving faster. God, please allow me to do my part.

The Unimaginable

As a grown woman thinking back to when I was young, I realize many things happened that I would have never imagined. In my youth, my path was clean with few detours. No kid thinks about red marks on their life plan. The Teacher didn't just write red X's. God tore out pages!

Little Nita would never have imagined being married more than once. I never would have written the fairytale romance with my Prince Charming being a crack addict. That's not how fairy tales work. I would not have imagined having a wonderful second husband only for him to die on me in my early fifties. Anita never imagined writing a book.

Never would I imagine my story having pages that I married a preacher. I would have thrown down the pen before writing that part of my saga. Anybody that knows me, know I don't like hats and I don't like shackles. To this day Anita does not wear hats, and I'm not hoity-toity.

I would not have imagined having only two kids and not four. I never would have imagined being excited to have grandchildren. I would have fully imagined not wanting to be called Grandma. My cool name for my grandkids to call me is Mysha (sounds like Mee sha). Mysha means happy for an entire life and a message bearer from God.

Here are my final reflections on my Mom, the unimaginable ancient. I didn't have a good frame of reference about growing old gradually and what that would look like on my Mom. Seeing her steps become fewer and her memories fade has put me atilt. I know my heart will shatter another shard when God sees fit to take her. God more than answered my prayer for a long life for my Mom. Thank you, Lord.

Like with Rev, when the time came to end suffering in exchange for eternal life, God knew best. I will trust God to do what is best for everyone's conclusion, even my Mom's. Anyone who has known me all my life could see something in me that was birthing. They could sense something. None of us, including me, could put our finger on it. God let my heart walk in so many other people's shoes along the way. My interpretation of other's shoes wasn't exact, but close enough. My heart was not one of a gladiator but of a heart full of compassion.

I have been in the ring many times, but the battle is not mine. I've been bloodied, but God has been with me every time. Sometimes I was too daft to know it. I am grateful for Him. I started off not wanting Him as part of my saga. Now I can't imagine Him, His Word, His Son, or His Spirit being anywhere but with me. I could never have imagined the pages He would write in my book.

My expressions to many audiences of strangers have been His tonic for the brokenhearted like my own. The best decision of my entire life has been to know Jesus Christ. To trust Him. To let the Father parent me.

Band-Aid for the Pain

As I'm drawing to the close of our journey, I want you to clearly understand that *pain* has strengthened me. Sometimes, going through direct hits by Satan, I've dropped to my knees saying, "I love you, God." The fiery arrows were meant to make me curse God. I received them and cried help me, Lord. I praise God and ask Him to hold me up and to cover me through raging waves. Like Peter sinking, I cry, "Save me." Jesus grabs me every time. The Spirit comforts and protects me every time. The Three in One carry me.

Pain has strengthened my faith. People, be careful what you wish for. Many want what they see as success. People in service to God are not successful; they are *tested*. Testing of your faith brings completeness and maturity. Nothing about trials comes without pain and suffering. If seeing my leaps doesn't help you see the choices, valleys, craters, cuts, and bruises, you need to start over with your good glasses.

Faith muscles don't magically happen like they do with characters on TV. Pain and real suffering forge giants in the faith who don't ask to be at head tables.

We have some secular legends and even they will admit that with success came pain. Check out the documentaries of Tyler Perry, Oprah Winfrey, Cicely Tyson, Shirley Chisholm, Medgar Evers, or Coretta Scott King. These people suffered. Name recognition and notoriety comes with a cost, sometimes even death.

The pain, fear, questioning or fortitude to marshal onward can't be covered with a Band-Aid. You can't *quit*. Quitting costs more than we can afford. None of us can give up on what God has purposed us to do. Behind the makeup, hair, and words, and so-called fame don't look past the pain.

I'm not being morbid or dark in what I'm telling you. Everything I have shared is not tainted because of grief. I believe grief has informed me. I believe failure, being a single parent, making a lifetime of bad decisions, and taking leaps have all made me stronger and the person I am now. My journey has been twisted and not straight. The detours have sometimes been a bitch. Fault the saga. Grief alone has been something. The other parts have been none too sugary.

In the pain, I didn't get extra credit for not calling hurt what it was. I had to do so much spiritual work for life, this book, and my progress. I had to cry out to God. I had to be real with Him. I have to be real with you.

I wasn't mad about God not miraculously healing Rev. I could have been like the millions of others are when their loved ones die. But I wasn't. I was thankful God extended his time when He could have taken him so many times before 2021. Grief programs all assume the anger. I didn't have it. I tried to find the anger, but I had so much gratefulness. I had a lot of hurt and missing my friend. There was no supersized Band-Aid for the pain. Years of healing will be ongoing for the work of this loss. He gave me comfort, or I should say He gave me the Comforter. It was the Comforter who surgically reapplied fibers back into my soul that pain cruelly pulled out.

Processing pain is not easy and for the faint of heart. Pain and recovery are not a cookie cutter solution. We all go through our trials differently. The operant word is *through*. Go through. Don't stagnate. Psalm 23 says when I go through the valley of the shadow of death, I will fear no evil. Push through!

Anita "The Work in Progress"

I've never had a problem with pushing. When it comes to the internal Anita challenges, I fight a lot of things. Here is a list of my battlegrounds of being: ambitious, prideful, critical, fearful, impatient, doubting, and about forty other that raise their hands for the list.

The thing about having gifts and talents from God is you have to know how to balance self-confidence. More than self-confidence there is self-reliance, selfish ambitious, knowing it all, and arrogance. For the most part I try to remain humble; however, I don't offer sessions on humility. I don't talk a lot about topics I am not a beacon of always demonstrating. David in the Bible wasn't tapped to build the tabernacle for all the blood on his hands. I suspect I wouldn't be tapped to give a conference on humility for the same premise. That's not the book you are reading.

I want to share that being a pusher does involve being self-motivated. I have made a lot of choices, being self-willed and fully motivated.

I have jumped out in the deep with questionable choices. Whether you use the word *choice* or *decision*, I made them and I had to go through the aches and pains in the recovery.

Here's evidence to show some befores and afters of my full circle moments: Before financial wisdom, I had credit reports hovering in the 500s, whereas after heeding wisdom, the report kissed the 800s. Before healthy nutrition, I was well over 200 pounds and with discipline I am less than 200 pounds. I struggle with emotional eating and that's a lifetime of inside work for me. The before-and-after list can go on for every part of my life where wisdom, discipline, patience, and wise counsel were exercised versus it was not. The prior chapters have demonstrated all of my befores and afters in one form or another.

I am a work in progress, and I have been called a pusher. Rev, not so long before he died, told Broderick as we were setting up for Bible study, "Anita is a pusher."

I was surprised. Broderick had just married our daughter a few months earlier in a private ceremony that Rev officiated. I didn't like what he said or how he said it. We had a long day at the infusion center. The nurse had just left our home. Rev was weak and we had minutes before starting a Bible class that he declared he wanted to do.

For me, if you want to have Bible class, logistical things and preparations need to happen. I didn't feel I was pushing; I thought I was preparing. Regardless, Rev said it and Broderick received it. Rev knew me best. I suspect he wanted his new son-in-law to know who I was but who Albani grew up under. Those tendencies were not lost on his oldest daughter.

The work in progress with me is I am a builder. If you tell me you want to do something and it's of the Lord, I will push for that. With God we can absolutely make lightning in a bottle. You may wonder why my tick tock in my head is getting so loud. Why now? I was up close and personal with death for two and a half weeks. Things in hospice slow life down and puts a "*perspective*" lens on life that those who have never experienced it do not appreciate.

I am familiar with the urgency of the dash as I haven't been before. What dash? Gravestones have a dash between the birth date and the death date. I don't want to leave anything on the table for the dash. I don't think about dying, but I do think about living as if tomorrow is not promised. It is not.

Rev used to read to us from a book of questions: would you like to know when you will die? I would always say *no*. My rationale was that I want to live like I don't know, but it could be tomorrow, so live today.

I'm an adventurer. I am curious. I love to learn and grow. I don't like living as though I'm going to stay in the twelfth grade for the rest of my life. I want to keep growing until I'm called *up*! God went all in for you and me. I'm stubborn enough to want to return the favor. My business is to spill my guts and share how God got me through and He can do the same and more for each of you. For the current, next, and future generations, I'm hoping when I leave here, I have left it all on the mat. Don't quit, don't give up, don't lose hope—fight until there's no more dash!

Who Is Anita?

My relationship with myself is healthy. If I've left any other impression, that would not be the truth. I love myself and I want all good things for me and ultimately for you. I spend time protecting that little girl Nita who was knocked off her balance from early childhood by cancer and my Dad dying.

My desires and fears come from that period of loss that many people experience. I'm sure the loss of my husband in 2021 will shape me and my girls. Death is a challenge in my life that informs me and the urgency of my relationship with myself and others. I love and care for people (starting with myself) as if there is not a tomorrow.

The relationship I have with myself is to live every day as though it could be my last. When I have an internal struggle, I ask if I have given my best, if I have loved, and, if today is it, have I lived so that God will say, "Well done." When facing all of the challenges inside, His "Well Done" is enough for me. That is the final outcome I seek.

Who is Anita, you may ask. My response some days is "Your guess is as good as mine." At this point, I suspect you are nodding. Depending on the day, I could be right there with you or have no clue. I can be a chameleon and be the woman behind the motif.

My constitution strives to be constant and genuine. I too fall into the persona of hiding behind good makeup and hair when I want to appear all together when I'm not. I want to be real with you, and that's why I'm not giving you hard, concrete answers. Some days I don't know. Every day is a new day. I pray to be discerning, loving, and open in all I do for the Lord. The outcome isn't always aces, but I keep trying.

The reality is that many people don't ask themselves who they are. As an interviewer, I probe and delve into others as I learn parts of myself from their lives. Who and what I am to myself is mine to answer. Who I am to you can be different.

I truly am a chameleon of sorts. I expand and contract for what's needed in the moment. That's true for what's needed for me or for others.

Here's some irony for you. I can be totally impatient inwardly and totally patient with people and situations outwardly. My family can tell when I'm focused and when I'm just tolerating. I don't join in a lot of conversations that are cyclical and going nowhere. I don't like sitting around talking about irrelevant things.

I'm outwardly open and extroverted in nature around some and then want to be left in a corner with others. When I get hold of interesting topics, whether reading, people, or a movie, I'm all in. I tune out the noise around me. People will ask a couple of times if I heard them. I'll say, "No. What did you say?" That's how much I can totally tune people and noise out.

I have switches. I switch on and off, depending on my interest. As I age, boy do my switches turn. As my time on the blue marble is turning, I want to turn my attention to what brings me peace and moments to exhale. That's who Anita is for the time being. Tick tock.

The Peace of My Leap

I celebrate peace and goodwill far more than Christmas. I am pretty good about having the Prince of Peace with me all year round. With my leaps and my life choices, I am at peace. I would be remiss if I didn't leave you with how I'm processing peace these days. Dear reading buddy, that's what we are if you have come this far. You and I have firmly established I'm no saint. You don't have to call me angel or anything grand given this reading. Like everybody, my peace can be flaky. I misplace it and need to click my heels twice to find it. I'm kidding. I only click once!

Seriously, moments come when I lose focus on important things for the trivial and temporary. I lose my peace when I find myself going after things I want but don't need. I've harped about tick tock and bigger vision, but when I am surrounded by childish things, childish thinking, and childish toys, I get distracted. What's important to God and what's important to me gets lost sometimes. My purpose and His call can take a back seat. That's jarring but the truth. Writing *A Leap of Faith* took discipline. It took saying no to things I wanted to say yes to. The journey of forcing flashbacks forced me to sacrifice comfort and fun. I had to say no in order to get to the bigger result of helping that one person who may need my story. If you are the one, I helped all of this has been worth the sacrifice.

I am hoping you have seen that you are not alone in the journey. I hope you will say if Anita can survive being the clown of her story, so can you. Clowns need love too. I hope you will have a little compassion for yourself. I hope every now and then you'll take that much needed exhale. Breathe.

Finding peace in your chaos is listening for the small, still voice of God saying He's there. I had to switch on my hearing aid to tune to His frequency, to listen for the needle to turn to His peace in the days of my storms. Here's the secret: you have to learn to listen on God's bandwidth of trust. I am finding more peace learning to trust God, not me. It sounds easy, but it's not. The issue, my new buddy, is not Him, but *me*.

Leaning not to my own understanding is the problem. Proverbs 3:5 trips me. I have to trust Him and not myself in the deeper plans of my life. I have to let go of the reins of my life for the unknowns. I have to trust Him in the weird directions of faith He takes me. Abram was good about leaving home with no map, Anita not so much. Even with my strong will, God is still good about giving me grace. He gives the order of GO and without change He doesn't budge until I move.

Geography and directions aren't my strong suit. Directions without knowledge rattle my peace. *Start a teaching podcast. Start speaking. Write a book. Go here. Move there.* All of it requires these new leaps, new depths, His plans. You will find me looking up to heaven saying, "God, what are you up to now?" He doesn't answer or budge. Anita, go.

I'm gaining calm in my freak-outs. You can't tell, but He can. The rebound is quicker. Without Rev, the initial leaps were terrifying. Don't throw me under the bus with your fear and faith lectures. New trips down unknown highways are scary for me. I'm gripping with tight knuckles to God and taking one foot in front of the other. I am gripping hard now and starting to swing back and forth as we walk through. He knows where He's leading me.

That's me growing up. I'm walking valleys, leaping out of boats, and moving from city to city with Him. I don't have it figured out. That's the beauty of this life. He never demanded that I have it all figured out. He wanted me to figure it out with Him, one day at a time.

So be like me and strive for contentment, wisdom, and faithfulness. Take the leap and grab hold to His neck! We'll get to the pearly gates. We'll scribble down some notes along the way. We'll laugh and cry some days. We'll cross the finish line. I know Christ loves me *through*. He has loved me *straight through*. Nothing questionable about that!

With love, I leave you in peace.

Anita

EPILOGUE

I love good writing and meaningful conversations. I hope our time together has been thought provoking. I hope you have found your experience with *A Leap of Faith* as introspective as writing it has been for me. With every flashback I endured, I hope you were touched by the experience.

I want you to know you are important to God. You reading this book was no accident. God has your undivided attention. Let Him draw closer to you.

If you listen to that small, still voice inside, you'll know He wants to get to know you. He wants to be part of your life. The best decision of my entire life has been my relationship with the friend Jesus Christ. What a journey to take your leap of faith toward Him.

By Faith

Top Left and Right: Rosetta and William Bush (Mom and Dad)

Middle Left and Right: Me and Dad

Bottom Center: Me

My Sister-Niece Collection

Top Left: Pam, Tina, and me. Top Right: Pam and me not so happy.

Middle Left: Me, Tina, and Pam.

Bottom Left: Tina, Pam, and Me.

Top Left: me, Middle School.

Top Right: Bush and me, Bumper cars (Amsterdam)

Middle Left: Me studying.

Middle Right: Me with outfit for Germany

Bottom left: Clara, me, and Mom HS Graduation

Top Left: Bridgewater Yearbook picture of Student Government
Executive Committee

Top Right: Bridgewater Yearbook picture of my friend Chelle and me

Bottom Left: Me holding ring before 1st Marriage

Top Left: Me and Albani.

Top Right: Mom and Albani

Middle Left: Albani (Dirt Road Disney).

Middle Right: Me and Albani

Bottom Left: Me receiving work honor

Rev and Me

Top Left: Albani and Faith (NICU).

Top Right: Me, Rev, Faith and Albani.

Middle Left: Albani, Rev and Faith.

Middle Right: Rev, Albani and Faith.

Bottom Left: Albani, Me and Faith.

Bottom Right: Faith and Albani (Dress up)

Top Left: Yvonne, Clara, Aaron (aka Bush), Me and Mom.

Top Right: Mom and Me.

Middle Left: Aaron (aka Bush), Yvonne, Me, Mom, Clara, and Wesley (Bush's son).

Middle Right: Aunt Vi, Aunt Betty and Mom

and Bottom Left: Aaron, Yvonne, Me, Clara, and Mom

Top Left: Faith, Albani, Broderick, David, Darlene, and Bridget

Top Right: Darlene, Rev, David, Timmy

Bottom Left: Me and Joyce

Bottom Right: Me, Joyce, and Darlene

Top Left: Broderick, Albani, Faith, Mom (94) and Me

Top Right: Faith, Me and Albani

Bottom Left: Faith and Albani

Bottom Right: Mom and Me